Praise for Amanda Wallingsford And *Embody Your Worth*

"A stirring, impactful book that helps break down the barriers of self-doubt and low self-esteem, *Embody Your Worth* empowers and motivates you to embrace your true worth. Drawing on a personal journey of hardship and transformation, Amanda Wallingsford's story will tug at your heartstrings and resonate with anyone seeking to unlock their potential. Brimming with practical exercises and advice, this book is a "must-read" for anyone eager to embark on a transformative journey of self-discovery and healing."

— Susan Friedmann, CSP, International Bestselling Author of *Riches in Niches: How to Make it BIG in a small Market*

"*Embody Your Worth* is a book we all need to read, digest, and apply to our daily lives. Whether you suffer from low self-esteem or you have spent years working on your personal development, you'll find strategies, practices, stories, and advice here that will make your life better. Amanda shares her powerful story of how she went from feeling worthless and that her loved ones would be better off with her dead to finding self-love, self-empowerment, and such serenity that even the worst of tragedies—the loss of her child—did not send her into a spiral. Read this book and be empowered!"

— Tyler R. Tichelaar, PhD and Award-Winning Author of *Narrow Lives* and *The Best Place*

"Amanda Wallingsford has provided readers with foundational theoretical underpinnings to explore one's self worth. In addition, she shares from her own personal life with authenticity and vulnerability. Her applied practice in the field of counseling gives her rich examples for readers to relate to in their own lives. The reflection questions and activities are thought-provoking and should prove insightful to the reader. I feel this book will help many in their personal life journeys and make way for the embracing of their self-worth and life dreams."

— Sharon L. Shields, PhD, Senior Associate Dean for Community and Special Projects, Vanderbilt University

"Make this book part of your own toolkit for mental health and well-being. I have read many, many books on personal growth and healing, yet *Embody Your Worth* has found a way to be unique and packed with so many useful and practical tools. As a therapist, I will be recommending this book to my clients. It is comprehensive, and I feel like Amanda is with me on every page, vulnerably sharing her story and encouragingly engaging me with her wisdom. There is so much rich information in this book. I love its layout, especially the Personal Reflection prompts. This book is amazing! The world needs this book now more than ever."

— Sarah Harris, LMFT-S, RPT-S, BC-TMH

Embody Your Worth

ESSENTIAL STRATEGIES TO LIVE CONFIDENTLY AND CREATE YOUR DREAM LIFE

Amanda Wallingsford LMFT-S

EMBODY YOUR WORTH
Essential Strategies to Live Confidently and Create Your Dream Life

Published by:

AVIVA PUBLISHING NEW YORK

Aviva Publishing
Lake Placid, NY
(518) 523-1320
www.AvivaPubs.com

Address all inquiries to:

Amanda Wallingsford
Amanda@EmbodyYourWorth.com
www.EmbodyYourWorth.com

ISBN: 978-1-63618-273-5 (hardcover)
ISBN: 978-1-63618-274-2 (paperback)
Library of Congress Control Number: 2023911003

Editing: Superior Book Productions
Cover Design & Interior Book Layout: Fusion Creative Works
Author Photo: Joi Conti

Every attempt has been made to properly source all quotes.

Printed in the United States of America

First Edition

2 4 6 8 10 12

Dedication

I dedicate this book to Ashton and Kailey.

Ashton, my precious angel,
may you live on in all the better parts of me.

Kailey, my sunshine, may you always see the beauty that I see in you.

Acknowledgments

To every person who saw the beauty in me when I could not see it myself, I extend my deepest gratitude. I would not be alive today to write this book were it not for you. To each of you who remained by my side during the darkest days of my life, from the bottom of my heart, thank you.

To Kevin, my soulmate, thank you for supporting me to follow the calling of writing this book. I appreciate the many sacrifices you made to help make this happen. But bigger than that, thank you for being the best life partner one could ask for. And thank you for inviting me into your life to be parents and role models to Kailey, Dalton, and Ashton. Kevin, Kailey, Dalton, and Ashton, you are the center of my dreams come true.

To Mom and Dad, there will never been enough words in the world to express my gratitude for every single thing you have done in my life to get me to where I am today. You have been there to hold me up when I have been in the deepest depths of despair. You have believed in me with each goal I set out to accomplish. You have taught me how to be a mother. And you have proven to me that unconditional love exists. Mom, thank you for dedicating every ounce of your being to providing me with the best life you could. Dad, thank you for being my hero. You are the best dad a child could ever wish for.

Thank you to each family member and friend who has shown so much enthusiasm and confidence in my ability to write this book. Your faith in me helped me keep my eye on the end goal and finish this to the end.

To Jaime Calle, thank you for seeing my beauty and reflecting it back to me, teaching me the tools to embody my worth, and modeling how to be a deeply effective therapist. You were the most instrumental person in helping me transform myself.

Thank you to my professor, mentor, and inspirational role model, Sharon Shields. You not only led the way to starting my career in social services, but you helped me rediscover my light that was in me all along.

Thank you to Alyssa Nobriga. You played such an important role in my healing after losing Ashton. Alyssa, I am a better person now because of you, your program, and the beautiful connections I made through you.

To all the clients who have granted me the opportunity to join you on your journey of navigating life, through times of pain, triumphs, and everything in between, thank you. I consider it my biggest privilege in life to be a part of your healing and growth. You have touched me in ways you will never know.

And last, but certainly not least, to Christine Gail and Tyler Tichelaar: As I work on the very last edits of this book before finally publishing, I have tears in my eyes as I feel gratitude for you two. Not only did you provide the professional support to get me to this point, but you helped me create something I am truly proud of and something that honors exactly what Ashton and God saw possible. From the bottom of my heart, thank you.

Contents

Introduction

"i think it's brave that you get up in the morning even if your soul is weary and your bones ache for rest.

i think it's brave that you keep on living
even if you don't know how to anymore.

i think it's brave that you push away the waves rolling in every day and you decide to fight.

i know there are days when you feel like giving up but
i think it's brave
that you never do."

— Lana Rafaela, "I Think It's Brave"

Am I Better Off Dead?

I remember one particular day during November of 1999 as though it were yesterday. I was on my way back to my dorm room after yet another class that I was barely making it through because just getting out of bed and facing life felt nearly impossible. As I paused my walk to look at the Student Counseling Center, an overwhelming feeling of being a complete burden to everyone in my life rushed over me. I felt so ashamed of myself that I couldn't get a hold of my depression. I had been crying every single day for months. I was having panic attacks regularly. I had recently started self-injuring, which terrified my family and friends. And my appetite had declined so badly that I had lost twenty pounds in the last three weeks. Nothing was helping me feel better about life. Then, standing there, the dreaded thought made its way in: *What if I am better off dead?* In a split second, having never had a suicidal thought before, I understood why people could take their own lives. My biological father and neighbor's deaths now made more sense to me.

Intellectually, I knew I had so many things going for me and so much to be thankful for. I was attending one of the best private universities in the country by earning a full-ride scholarship. My parents—my mom and my adoptive dad, Bob, whom I consider to be my "Dad"—were very supportive and would do anything to help me feel happy and succeed. I had many friends who had thus far proven themselves willing to go to significant lengths to help me feel loved and wanted.

Emotionally, I felt completely worthless. I believed I was insignificant. I felt permanently damaged because I heard from so many sources "You can choose to be happy." Yet, I couldn't figure it out. As a result, I felt so selfish that all the good I had in life wasn't enough to make me happy. I believed this made me a burden to those who loved me. I wondered if it was time for me to leave this earth permanently.

At that moment, I knew I really needed to get help.

The Circle of Life

On February 6, 2020, twenty-two years to the day after my biological father had died, I was in the hospital at thirty-four weeks pregnant with my only biological child, Ashton. At this point, I had been on bedrest for two weeks due to my water breaking too early. The doctors had been strategizing about when to induce labor, but the decision became clear during the daily ultrasound that indicated Ashton now had fluid in his lungs. The doctors came in around 7 p.m. to state it was "go time." While I did not want Ashton to have the same birthdate as my father's death date, I had this small sense of the miracle of life coming full circle. I felt this sense of calm and gratitude that I would be blessed with this little boy after enduring years of heartache.

Ashton arrived on the morning of February 7, 2020. Truly, he was a miracle baby. My husband, Kevin, and I were previously told at the eleventh week ultrasound that something was wrong with him and he would not survive another week. One doctor even suggested we induce a miscarriage because there was "no chance" of survival. But Kevin and I decided to see what God had planned for Ashton while we had tests run to determine the problem. We learned he had a genetic abnormality called Noonan syndrome.

Ashton proved that doctor quite wrong because he, sure enough, came out of my body alive and breathing!

He immediately went to the NICU (Neonatal Intensive Care Unit) as we anticipated he would. We were so elated that he had made it to birth, albeit six weeks early, that we were mentally planning to take him home after about six weeks in the hospital. He was such a fighter, making it to birth despite the odds, that Kevin and I knew he would be okay.

I Will Be Okay

On May 14, 2020, Ashton was ninety-eight days old. He had spent every day in the hospital since he was born. Complications caused by Noonan syndrome had overtaken his body, so his organs were starting to shut down. Every doctor and nurse had done everything they could over the course of his life to try to heal his body. Ashton had fought as hard as he could.

On this day, Kevin and I knew it was time to set him free. We held him as he took his last breath and his heart beat for the last time while all machines were removed from his body.

This became both the most heart-wrenching and indescribably beautiful moment of my entire life.

And yet as I held my precious baby boy to say goodbye, I knew I was going to be okay. I knew this would not break me. I felt the oddest sense of peace at the same time that my heart broke into a million little pieces.

Thank You, Baby Boy

October of 2020 came around. I had been grieving my biggest loss for five months and was learning how to live a "new normal" without my child. At the same time, I couldn't stop wondering how I truly was okay. I became extremely curious about my ability to cope so well. I was able to get out of bed and be productive. I was back to work full-time. My love and connection to Kevin and my stepdaughter were stronger than ever. I was able to laugh with my family and friends. Perhaps most importantly, I continued to feel gratitude for the life I had even without Ashton in physical form. The inner sense of peace I worked for years to find was still present every day.

How had I not gone back into a deep hole of depression? How did I know that losing Ashton was not because I deserved bad things? If this had happened fifteen years earlier, I would have been stuck in a spiral of questioning what I had done so wrong in my life to deserve to lose my father and then my child. I would have believed it was all my fault.

After pondering these questions and reflecting on my personal changes, I realized I am okay because I finally learned to truly love myself and see my worth. I learned that my worth is not attached to the unfairness of this tragedy. I learned that my worth cannot be measured nor can it be taken away.

So the next question was: *How* did I get from a place of complete self-loathing twenty years ago to knowing my true value?

As I asked myself this question, I heard Ashton telling me, "Mommy, continue to help others. Help them get to where you are. They can learn so much from you." So, it is because of my precious baby boy that I began the journey of writing this book.

Thank you, baby boy, for showing me the way.

Dear Reader, I See You

February 19, 2023

I sit here writing the very last section of this book. I have spent the last two-and-a-half years pouring my heart and soul into this. I followed Ashton's prompting to let my story and life lessons be a potential part of this survival guide for you, the reader.

Since you picked up this book, it tells me some part or much of you does not see your full worth. I want you to know that I see you. You are not alone. I see your pain. I understand your doubts. I've grappled with the same questions. I can relate to your confusion, trying to make sense of who you are and your place in this world.

I also see your beauty. I see your capabilities. I know you are as deserving of love and respect as any other human. I know you can heal the wounds that made you feel less than amazing. I believe in you. You, too, can create a life you love filled with joy, connection, purpose, and peace.

An Overview of My Life Journey

Some people who know me will see that I have written a book about how to live confidently and love yourself, and they are going to legitimately wonder how I, Amanda, could possibly be teaching others on this topic. These people knew me as a child or a young adult, but they do not know me now. They will rightfully wonder who I am now because they knew me when I had zero confidence or trust in my worth. They will know the Amanda who never felt important, couldn't see her own beauty, and felt dispensable.

I don't remember ever believing in myself as a child. I learned to believe in my achievements, yes. But I didn't believe I was good enough for others to value.

Because my entire education and career has been about learning to understand human psychology, I know my lack of self-worth originated from my biological father, Lee, being sporadically involved in my life starting at the age of two when he and my mom divorced. I questioned why I wasn't important enough for him to call me on my birthdays or come visit me more often than every couple of years. He told me he loved me whenever we did communicate, but I couldn't make sense of why he wouldn't show it more. While I felt grateful for my mom and dad's (Bob) care for me, how a biological parent could not want to be with their child didn't make sense to me. This left me feeling like something was inherently wrong with me. The idea that something must be wrong with me eventually became my answer to the question, "Why is he not around?"

As a child, I learned to "find" my worth by excelling in school and extracurricular activities. I solidified my worth by supporting others. I intuitively learned from Lee that people are often struggling inside, so I made it my mission to try to help everyone feel loved and appreciated. Supporting others became a central part of my identity and subconsciously became my strategy of ensuring my value and belonging in people's lives.

My heart hurt tremendously by the time I was in high school because Lee had become less and less involved in my life and had moved on to raise two other children. Then, during my freshman year, I experienced my first traumatic event. My next-door neighbor, whom I looked up to because of his joyful spirit and loving demeanor (he was the complete opposite of Lee), took his life. His suicide shocked everyone he knew because he appeared to be so happy. I could not wrap my mind around how someone like him could do this.

At that time (1994), "trauma" was not a thing, so no one knew how deeply the loss would exacerbate the pain I was already feeling. I learned to cope on my own, which included becoming the most reliable and available neighbor possible to his wife and two daughters. I made it my mission to be there for them in every way possible. While I struggled to understand Lee's inconsistency and emotional withdrawal, my own self-worth, and my neighbor's shocking death, I pushed through all the pain by excelling even more. Underneath the outer portrayal of succeeding in life, my undiagnosed depression, anxiety, and PTSD were brewing.

Five-and-a-half years after the traumatic loss of my neighbor, during my freshman year of college, I was continuing to push forward in life while my depression carried on under the surface. But on Saturday, February 7, 1998, my mom called and delivered devastating news. She informed me that my biological father, Lee, had killed himself the day before. And he had done it the same way my neighbor had.

At that moment, my life, at nineteen, was turned completely upside down and changed forever.

To cope with this second traumatic event, I continued to trudge forward by focusing on school and attempting to enjoy college life. I had already declared a major that would pave the way to becoming a counselor to people who experience hardship. I became even more committed to the cause of supporting people who struggled with depression or the negative effects of adverse life experiences.

Ironically, I didn't get counseling myself. As a result, I began to implode. I had made some incredible friends at college and remained great friends with people from high school. But my sense of worthlessness grew stronger and deeper. I felt like I didn't deserve any of my friends. Many of them tried to convince me of my worth, but I didn't believe them.

Two years later, my undiagnosed PTSD, depression, and anxiety finally took over my life. I no longer had it in me to be strong and keep fighting. I reached a point where I decided to take a small handful of Xanax after experiencing yet another horrible panic attack and fearing I was incapable of getting better. That night, I thought, *God, if I wake up from this tomorrow, then I am going to take it as a sign to be alive, and I will work my hardest to get through this treacherous pain.*

I woke up the next day.

And that is when my true healing journey began. I figured if I were going to follow my dreams of helping others, I better figure out how to help myself first.

My goal wasn't to find happiness. I knew happiness was a temporary, conditional emotion. I sought to find inner peace—peace that would help me weather any future storm that would inevitably come my way. And I had a feeling the way to get there was to discover my value.

My Professional Journey

I have been in the helping field for more than twenty years now. I began my career in social services as a residential counselor and then moved into case management. Within a few short years, I built my way up into leadership positions running various programs. I eventually returned to graduate school to become a marriage and family therapist in 2006 and earned my license in 2012.

Over the last twenty-four years, I have spent seventeen years in non-profit organizations working with youth and their families. I have been in a leadership or supervisory role for about fifteen of those years. I have owned my own private practice for approximately eight years. Throughout this time, I have been extensively trained in working with those who have experienced trauma. I am EMDR certified and trained in both trauma-focused cognitive behavior therapy and trauma conscious yoga method. I have recently also become a life transformation coach trained by the Institute for Coaching Mastery.

In my estimation, I have worked with more than 1,500 people and spent a minimum of 10,000 hours in service with people (directly spending time with them). Being in the room with this many hearts and minds has given me a wealth of understanding regarding the human experience and how people operate. My clients have taught me more than any book I have read or class I have taken.

My second best teacher has been the work I have done personally for my own healing and growth. Ever since that lowest low in 2000, I have remained committed to my well-being. This means that as a healer, I don't just talk the talk.

I walk the walk.

Everything I offer in this book is informed by my professional experience and my personal use of the tools. I don't include anything I haven't tried for myself. I won't suggest anything I won't do for myself. I share what I know works.

How This Book Is Organized

When I began to reflect on how I got to the place of knowing my worth and standing in my power, I typed out a summary of all the different lessons I had learned since my healing journey began twenty-some years ago. I named who helped me and how. From that emerged seven major themes that became the chapters in this book.

The first theme you will learn about, in Chapter 1, is how to embrace your humanity. I will provide some education on how the human body and mind function so you will better understand yourself. I will focus on the act of being loving and compassionate with yourself, particularly so you can give grace to the imperfections of being human. I set the stage for you to see yourself through a lens of realistic expectations while being empathetic with yourself.

In Chapter 2, you will learn about the survival strategies humans use to cope through life. This chapter will give you a deeper understanding of why you operate the way you do. You'll be given an opportunity to explore which strategies you want to hold onto and which you want to modify at this point in your development.

In Chapter 3, we will focus on the way you talk to yourself. You will learn solid techniques to repattern how you talk to yourself so your internal dialogue aligns with treating you as though you are worthy and special.

It's one thing to say, "Think positive." But doing so entails having a set of tools, so if you have conditioned thinking patterns that work against you, you will learn strategies to help you treat yourself as a best friend rather than an enemy.

Chapter 4 follows with helping you recognize your strengths and qualities. You absolutely have unique attributes and gifts that make you special. I want you to be able to see and believe these wholeheartedly for yourself. So we will explore what makes you the amazing person you are.

Chapter 5 dives into valuable strategies that will help you stand in your power as a human deserving of love and respect. You will learn various strategies to embody your worth through setting the standards of how others can treat you. You will learn about the Responsibility Backpack, a concept to help you become clear on the boundaries you have the right to set and what you are capable of being responsible for.

In Chapter 6, we will then weave in techniques for building healthy relationships. Relationships are possibly the most powerful avenues to deep healing when they are healthy for you. I will provide you with essential concepts to understand so you can move forward in building healthy relationships or work toward modifying relationships that already exist. You will learn some valuable communication nuts and bolts, which are foundational tools for creating healthy relationships.

The culmination of all these tools is the final strategy to help you fully embody your worth: understanding the power of your life choices. Chapter 7 is meant to help you feel empowered with what you can choose to do moving forward from this point. Recognizing your choices in each moment of your life will help you live consciously and toward alignment of what is best for you given what you know at the moment.

I will then round out everything you have learned and worked on by providing you with options on how you can further your healing toolbox. I will summarize various healing methods that exist so you can make an action plan around what will serve you best in your next chapter of growth. I will list resources I recommend based on my experience and knowledge. Your evolution will always be a work in progress so you can feel into what would be best for you during your next phase.

Chapter Structure

I open each chapter by sharing a personal story that illustrates what life looked like when I struggled with that chapter's topic. I then illustrate what life can look like as a result of applying the tools within the chapters. I want you to be able to envision what is possible.

I have designed this book to be not just something you skim over and later forget. As I wrote this book, I thought about what I wished I could have accessed in written form when I was struggling so I could learn how to apply the strategies. Therefore, I purposely include opportunities for you to integrate the concepts into your daily life. I do this through describing fictional scenarios (with fictional characters) that depict the topic at hand and then asking processing questions (named Scenario Reflection). I also invite you to reflect on your personal application of the concept in the section labeled Personal Reflection. Occasionally, I also include suggestions for you to complete a specific activity to apply a concept. You will see this labeled as Growth Activity. I envision you will get the most out of this book by using a journal or notebook and dedicating time to reflect and absorb the information.

Although I have written the book in the order that potentially makes the most sense to learn, the reality is we do not learn life lessons in a strict order. Life just doesn't happen that way. Therefore, another option is for you to search the Table of Content and go straight to a desired chapter when you are struggling in a particular area of your life. For example, imagine you plan to have a difficult conversation with someone soon and want guidance on how to make sure you take care of your own needs. You could then go to Chapter 5, which includes ways to set boundaries with others. There is no right or wrong way to take from this book what you need.

The last idea I have for how you can best use this book is to read the book in its entirety for the initial knowledge overview and then go back to the parts of the book where you want to dive deeper in your skill development. This may be the first time you have heard of some of these concepts and tools. Or you may read something you have heard before, but you never knew how to take that knowledge further. Whatever fits for you, please use it. My growth, as you will read, did not happen in linear fashion. And I didn't just take a crash course in self-worth and, poof, I was changed. You will ebb and flow, just as I have, through your lessons and growth.

My Hopes for You as You Read This Book

When I was a senior in college, I couldn't get the image out of my mind of my life being a canvas. At the time, that canvas felt as though it primarily consisted of shades of gray. It seemed to have minimal color. Yet I was intent on learning to add color to the canvas each day.

My hope as you read this book is that you will see what is possible for you. I wish for you to see that you can add color to your canvas by learning and then implementing the tools in this book. I hope you see yourself in me or the fictional characters so you will feel less alone and understood. I never would have bet all the money in the world all those years ago that I would grow into the person I am today because I did not see it as possible. As my best therapist once said to me, "Your self-esteem was at a -80 when we started our work together." If I can arrive at this point in my life knowing my worth and feeling peace amid another tragedy, then I know it is possible for you as well.

My next hope is you will be kind and patient with yourself as you read. I want you to learn to meet yourself where you are in the here and now. I hope you learn to cherish being *perfectly imperfect* at each step throughout your healing and growth journey. May you extend love to yourself as you practice and implement the strategies, just as you would extend love to an eager, innocent child learning to walk. Self-growth is a process, so please be patient with yourself.

My last hope is you will feel empowered to embody that amazing person you are. Learn to embrace your most authentic self that aligns with your values and dreams. Practice standing in your worth until it's not practice any more. Realize that the short-term discomfort of trying new ways of being will absolutely be worth the long-term gains. Step into all you are worth so you can build that life you dream of. Become the masterpiece you are destined to be!

I wish you much good fortune, comfort, life-changing realizations, and peace as you engage in this journey with me.

~Amanda Wallingford

CHAPTER 1

Embracing Your Humanity

"There is a crack in everything. That's how the light gets in."
— Leonard Cohen

It's August 2000, and I have just started my senior year of college. I'm sitting on the windowsill of my dorm room looking out the window at the dorm next to mine. I can see the suite I lived in with five other girls during the first semester of last year. This year I am living alone. With tears rolling down my face, I am reminded of how these girls won't speak to me anymore. I also think of the best friends I had last year who decided to end our relationships.

As I feel the pain of the rejection and loss, I am torn about why it all happened. My mind knows it wasn't my fault that I became so incredibly depressed last year that I lashed out in unhealthy ways. I logically know I went through extremely challenging circumstances that caused my body and mind to deteriorate. After all, mounds of research show children who experience parental abandonment or lose loved ones to suicide are likely to experience mental health issues.

Yet, I can't stop thinking that everything was my fault because I *let* my depression get so bad. Images of times when I was too much to handle with my meltdowns, panic attacks, and outbursts run through my mind. My thoughts bounce back and forth between, *It wasn't my fault I got so sick*, and *I should have known and done better. I deserve to be alone now.* I feel the despair and confusion of losing my friends pounding in my chest. I continue to question my worth and value. I believe I am inherently broken.

But then I take a deep breath and tune into that flicker of light in my gut that has always been a part of me. This light, although I don't understand where it came from, fuels my determination to keep going.

I shift my focus to my decision to return to Vanderbilt to finish my degree despite losing my closest friends. I know I am doing this for me and no one else. I'm aware that I don't fully love myself right now, and I feel tremendous shame over my behavior last year, but I am committed to continuing to learn to love myself. I know I need to learn to do so to build the life I desire because I *never* want to be in the position of contemplating suicide again.

The Development of Self-Worth

I invite you right now to look outside and try to spot a bird. Observe this beautiful animal for a few minutes. Notice the simplicity of its life. Its few tasks for the day include drinking water, finding food, sleeping, and dispelling its waste. It might have the added responsibility of protecting its offspring. And, ultimately, it has the major task of avoiding danger to stay alive.

As a human, you are different. Yes, you have survival tasks such as eating, sleeping, and dispelling waste. But unlike other species, you have the ability to think abstractly. You experience emotions. You seek fulfillment and happiness. You create stories about why things happen and what events mean. You even question the value of your existence. Your capabilities as a human add layers of complexity to life.

Do you think the bird you observed ever sits on a tree branch and says to itself, "Wow, I am a complete failure!" or conversely, "Yes! I am so proud of myself!"? Of course, it doesn't. It's not built to do this.

Self-worth is a subjective experience unique to humans. If you love yourself, it is because you have somehow been provided the framework and reinforcement to see yourself as capable, loved, and safe. Your needs have been met consistently. And people have communicated that your worth is separate from how you act.

So, how does the sense of self go awry? How do you arrive at the conclusion you are unworthy, broken, or unlovable? What makes you believe you are not good enough or deserve less than other humans? Where do you get the idea you don't belong?

The answers comes down to one thing: Somewhere along the way, you received or interpreted the message that something is wrong with you. You didn't just wake up one day and decide not to love yourself, did you? Something happened to lead you to the conclusion that you are somehow less than worthy. And typically, it happened or began in childhood.

There are so many situations and circumstances that could lead you to believe something is wrong with you. I could never write a complete list of the causes because there are too many to name and too many varying factors. However, I do want to name a few that have a high probability of damage to your sense of worth:

- Experiencing any type of abuse that jeopardized your physical or emotional safety.
- Being raised by emotionally immature caregivers who did not know how to provide unconditional love.
- Experiencing parental/caregiver absence or inconsistent participation in your life.
- Learning from your environment that your worth is earned rather than inherent.
- Being teased, ostracized, or bullied by others (including peers).
- Experiencing a traumatic event (or series of events) that shifts your view of yourself in this world.

Whatever the cause, if you struggle to know your value, your experience is valid and we will work toward rebuilding your sense of self throughout this book.

Being Human

Most of us live in a culture that denies what it means to be human. Children are told not to cry when they get hurt. Professionals are expected to work until they drop. News outlets display constant images of horrible events as if no one will have a physiological stress response to the events. In so many ways, you are expected to be superhuman or not human at all.

To begin the journey of embodying your worth, you must start by recognizing how you function as a human. I want you to learn that you operate *just as you are designed* as a human.

My self-criticism journey began at a young age, but my self-loathing hit its worst point when my mental health crashed during my junior year of college. At the time, there was limited understanding of depression and anxiety. There was even less knowledge of the effects of trauma or adverse life experiences. "Trauma" was only recognized in combat veterans, and only if they exhibited extreme symptoms of post-traumatic stress disorder (PTSD). If there had been more knowledge back then, my depression and anxiety might have been diagnosed as early as age twelve. But no one in my life knew better. When I sought clinical help for the first time during my junior year of college, someone should have recognized I was experiencing PTSD. But because of the mental health information available at the time, I was diagnosed with depression caused by grief. At the time, I seriously thought I was crazy. I thought I had completely lost my marbles. I imagine some other people did too. It took years for a professional to recognize I had been experiencing numerous PTSD symptoms since I was fourteen after my neighbor died. Because my father died in the same manner as my neighbor, my symptoms worsened. I became stuck in hypervigilance mode all day every day, regularly imagined disturbing images of my father and neighbor and their violent final moments, and felt terrified on a daily basis that more of my loved ones would die tragically.

Here is what I wish I knew then but didn't learn until years later when I was studying trauma as a professional: My brain and body were reacting *exactly* as they were designed in response to my stressful and traumatic life events. Eventually, my body became stuck in trauma response mode because my experiences had not been treated along the way.

Currently when clients begin therapy with me, many are often just as clueless as I was all those years ago (even though it is twenty years later and the information is out there). When I explain the following functions, they feel shocked and relieved that their body is designed to function in the way they deem abnormal and crazy. Therefore, I anticipate that this information will be valuable to you as well.

Brain Development

Fascinatingly, when you are born, your brain has all the brain cells (neurons) it will have for the rest of your life.[1] What doesn't yet exist are the connections between the cells. Making connections between cells leads to your development. Connections are made through factors such as exposure to new situations, nutrition, and reinforcement.

For the most part, the brain cannot fast forward its development. Certain developmental tasks take place at general ages due to the chronological building of cell connections. For example, you cannot bombard a six-month-old baby with language over the course of one month and then expect it suddenly to hold an adult conversation.

The entire brain develops from the bottom (the section right above the spinal cord) to top (near the forehead). The brainstem is the first to begin developing, starting in-utero. This part of the brain is responsible for the body's involuntary processes that preserve life. Brainstem tasks include

1 https://www.firstthingsfirst.org/early-childhood-matters/brain-development/. Accessed March 9, 2023.

regulating breathing, keeping the heart pumping, and processing audio and visual cues. Expanding from the brainstem, other parts of our brain develop at different stages of life.

The cerebellum is responsible for physical movement, body posture (including equilibrium), and speech. This development begins in utero and continues over the first few years of a child's life. The limbic system, which is primarily responsible for emotional regulation and memory, does most of its development during adolescence. This is integral in the formation of self-worth due to how the brain emotionally experiences life events, which interplays with how the brain makes meaning of events.

The last part of the brain to develop is the cerebral cortex. This part of the brain separates our species from others. It is responsible for advanced thinking, such as imagination, language, perception, and reasoning. It is the home of complex and abstract thinking. The cerebral cortex interprets and gives meaning to life events. Research shows that this part of our brain doesn't reach full maturity until approximately age twenty-five.[2]

All parts of the brain are designed to grow and work in tandem over time. I like to think of the parts of the brain as being like a football team. On a football team, all the positions come together to play the game. While some positions are more independent (such as the kicker coming in only at designated times), the majority of the positions are interdependent. The quarterback starts the play and is responsible for directing the team on the field, but the team members still need to communicate and work together. Football teams also ideally get better over time as they practice together. The brain is similar. As the parts develop and work together over time, the person matures and becomes more capable.

If stress occurs in a developing brain, each part's development is likely to be affected. Certain parts of the brain may develop later than average or parts may not communicate efficiently or effectively. Research on stress

2 https://www.ncbi.nlm.nih.gov/pmc/articles/PMC3621648/. Accessed March 11, 2023.

in humans and its effect on brain development is quite extensive. While I won't discuss it in detail in this book, suffice it to say that if a child's brain develops in situations that threaten emotional or physical safety, sections of the brain are likely to be compromised and may require longer and more direct developmental support to function at optimal levels.

If your self-worth was damaged by childhood stressors, the stress you went through most likely surpassed your developmental capacity. The younger you were when you went through the stressors, the less ability your brain had to make sense of the situation and respond in optimal ways. Further, if you had little to no caregiver support during stressful times, then no one was there to teach you how to cope well. As a result, you were put in a position to handle more than your little mind was capable of.

The good news: The brain has an incredible capacity to heal and rewire. It makes thousands of new connections every minute. The tools throughout this book will assist you in rewiring your brain to help you through self-worth struggles.

Personal Reflection

Looking back on your childhood, what situations did you face that were beyond your developmental capacity? What information were you incapable of knowing at the time due to being too young to understand and/or due to not having someone to share that information or knowledge with? If you get stuck on this reflection, think of a child you know and whether you would expect them to know how to handle what you were asked to handle.

Human Stress Response

Regardless of the brain's developmental stage or how many cells are talking to each other, the brain's ultimate task is to keep you alive. To do so, your brain must be able to detect threats and then communicate how to respond to the rest of your body.

Humans and many other species operate through the functions of the *nervous system.* Your nervous system includes your brain, spinal cord, and nerves. The nervous system is responsible for sending messages between the brain and the body. It enables the parts of the body to operate together like when your lungs take deeper breaths as you are running.

An extremely powerful part of our brain is the amygdala. It is the starting point for detecting danger and telling the rest of the nervous system to take action. The amygdala saves our lives.

The amygdala is essentially our brain's smoke detector (a term coined by trauma specialist Bessel van der Kolk).[3] When a threat is detected (real or perceived), the smoke detector goes off, sending alarm signals to tell the body to respond to the threat. Thus, the human stress response is activated. According to the Center for Integrated Health, "The stress response… is the emergency reaction system of the body."[4]

When we are not responding to stress, we are in what's called "rest and digest" mode. In other words, our body is cruising along feeling calm. When our nervous system is regulated, we think straight, have control of our emotions and reactions, and can make sound assessments and decisions about what is going on. This is the state we aim for at all times.

When the amygdala interprets a cue to mean we are in (potential) danger, our stress system activates, and our nervous system goes into fight, flight, or freeze mode so our body can take appropriate action to defend against the threat. In fight or flight mode, our blood pressure and heart rate increase, we release adrenaline, and we increase oxygenation to the organs among other responses. These changes help the body defend against the threat (fight) or get away (flee). Imagine you see a heavy piece of machin-

---

3 Van der Kolk, Bessel. *The Body Keeps the Score*. New York, NY: Penguin, 2014. p. 30.

4 https://www.mirecc.va.gov/cih-visn2/Documents/Patient_Education_Handouts/Stress_Response_and_How_It_Can_Affect_You_Version_3.pdf. Accessed March 9, 2023.

ery fall on someone's leg. Your system might respond rapidly to try to lift the machinery off. This is an example of fight mode. Your system accesses increased strength and rapid response to "fight off" the threat. If someone appears about to lunge at you, you also need your body to kick into high gear to get away or "flee." This response system is valuable when the situation *warrants* a fight or flight response.

The third response, to freeze, is to become immobile. This freeze response is valuable for animals to either remain still and avoid detection from predators or play dead to mislead a predator.[5] The freeze state in other animals can be crucial to survival. In humans, the freeze response is valuable in a few circumstances, but it becomes ineffective when a situation does not warrant a freeze response or when the body gets stuck in this state.

When our fight, flight, or freeze response is activated, our system is designed to shut off communication to other parts of our brain, such as our emotional center that are deemed unnecessary at the time of the experienced threat. Prolonged defensive responses can lead to emotional dysregulation, undermining our ability to think clearly or operate effectively. We might be less able to form cohesive thoughts, manage our emotions, or make wise decisions. This is because the sole purpose of the heightened response is to keep us safe and alive. If we are experiencing actual danger, it is dangerous to get caught up in our emotions or wondering why someone might be threatening us with a knife. This works well in some situations and works very well for less developed species. However, when we are repeatedly in an unwarranted fight, flight, or freeze state, it causes significant stress.

What I think is most important to understand here is if you have been in a situation that triggered your nervous system to go into any of these modes, it is perfectly normal for your body to respond similarly in the future even if the situation does not require the activated response. That means the amygdala is doing its job because it is designed to remember

5 Levine, Peter A. *Healing Trauma.* Boulder, CO: Sounds True, 2008. p. 28-9.

potential threats. Therefore, absolutely nothing is wrong with you, your body, or your brain. Your body is responding *exactly* the way it is designed.

Trauma Response

Trauma is a common part of conversations today. This was not the case even ten years ago. I find it amazing that people are now more aware of trauma and willing to talk about traumatic experiences. I do find, however, that many still lack understanding of what trauma is and why it is important to recognize your own trauma.

Broadly defined, trauma is "a deeply distressing or disturbing experience." By this definition, most people have been through some sort of trauma. It is hard for anyone to get through life without this kind of experience.

SAMHSA, the Substance Abuse and Mental Health Services Administration of the US Federal Government, describes individual trauma as resulting from an event, series of events, or set of circumstances that is experienced by an individual as physically or emotionally harmful or life threatening and that has lasting adverse effects on the individual's functioning and mental, physical, social, emotional, or spiritual well-being.[6]

I was taught to think of trauma in terms of an event (or series of events) that was so disturbing or distressing it shifted your view of the world and/or of yourself. It often comes with a before and after awareness of how you experience the world. You might be able to pinpoint this shift depending on your mental maturity. As an example, perhaps someone historically feels safe walking to work. But one day, a truck loses control during a rainstorm and nearly hits them. From that point on, that person may no longer feel safe walking to work.

Events can still be traumatic if they happened so early developmentally that you do not remember the before-and-after shift. For example, suppose a child loves dogs. Then at three, they are playing alone outside and a dog bites them so badly they have to be rushed to the hospital to get the

6 https://www.samhsa.gov/trauma-violence#. Accessed March 9, 2023.

wound stitched up. From that point forward, the child is scared of dogs and scared of playing outside by themselves. The world is no longer safe in this child's eyes.

In addition, trauma is relative to each person. What is not traumatic for one person can be traumatic for the next. For example, people get into car accidents daily. Yet car accidents are not traumatic for everyone. Trauma is defined by individual experience. Because of this, there is not a list of traumatic events. Only the person who has the experience gets to determine if it qualifies as traumatic. This applies to you as well. No one but *you* gets to define your trauma.

This individual experience is often closely tied to how the body responds to the event. Traumatic response occurs when the event is so significant the body gets stuck in the fight, flight, or freeze response. The amygdala is designed to remember any cue of such a significant event so it can prepare to respond if the threat cues arise again. However, if the body stays in any of these states, then the body is stuck in traumatic response. At that point, a diagnosis of post-traumatic stress disorder might apply. Official medical diagnoses are determined by the *Diagnostic and Statistical Manual of Mental Disorders,* fifth edition, text revision (DSM-5-TR).

You might not meet the full PTSD criteria to be medically diagnosed, but you can still experience residual traumatic physiological responses. One such response is hypervigilance, defined as "the elevated state of constantly assessing potential threats around you."[7] This definition makes sense because it is the body's way of being on high alert for danger. Since the body is designed to look out for threats, it can take time and support to teach the body it can settle down again (return to rest and digest).

Aside from traumatic physiological responses, the mind will learn to adapt behaviors to be on the lookout for future threats based on your new worldview. For example, an adult who experienced childhood poverty

---

7 https://www.webmd.com/mental-health/what-is-hypervigilance. Accessed March 9, 2023.

and homelessness might develop the habit of overworking to earn overtime to avoid struggling to meet basic needs ever again. If you have been through trauma and don't understand it as trauma or understand how it has changed your worldview, you might see yourself as abnormal, broken, or dysfunctional. But when you learn to understand yourself through the lens of the natural human trauma response, you can see you are responding exactly as you are designed.

Trauma can take a while to work through and heal from. In Chapter 8, you will find a list of resources to help. At the same time, you will also discover that the majority of the tools in this book are also effective in assisting you in your journey of healing and growing.

Implicit and Explicit Information

We are almost always processing information. As we sort it, our brain splits information into two categories. The first is explicit information, which is information expressed directly and clearly. With this type of information, there is no confusion. A clear sky explicitly indicates rainless weather because rain cannot be produced without clouds. A nurse who says, "I will be providing your care," is communicating explicitly about being the assigned provider to the patient. The majority of the content in this book is explicit information because I am being direct and deliberate with the words I use to minimize misinterpretation.

Implicit information, on the other hand, is indirect, vague, or ambiguous. Nonverbal communication, such as body posture or tone of voice, is a form of implied information. We use reasoning skills to deduce the meaning of implicit information. For example, if someone shouts really loud and slams their fist on a table, their behavior may imply they are angry. When someone waves their hand toward you, you might infer it means they are saying hello. The biggest challenge with implicit information is that people can interpret it in different ways. To someone else, the person waving their hand might be signaling for someone to come toward them rather than just saying hello.

The lens through which we experience life is largely created by the meanings we assign to implied information. The meanings we assign to people's behavior and to life events directly influence the meanings we assign to ourselves and our value.

The way we see ourselves based on implied messages begins in childhood before we can even talk. The best way to demonstrate how this plays out is to give examples.

> *Ana is a seven-year-old girl who spends a lot of time with her grandma and grandpa after school. She has directly heard her grandparents say multiple times, "Treat everyone with kindness. Everyone matters." However, she observes that when her grandparents approach a person with light skin, they smile, look them directly in the eyes, and say hello. On the contrary, she notices that whenever her grandparents pass by a person with brown skin, they look the other way and say nothing.*

The explicit message Ana received was through her grandparents' words. However, the implicit message she learned by observation of their behavior was that people with white skin should be treated with more kindness than people with brown skin. What she sees her grandparents do will affect her behavior more than what they say.

> *Noah is a five-year-old who lives with his mom. She tells him "I love you" often and says that she "would do anything for him." But nearly every weekend, she gets drunk and hits him, causing physical injury.*

Noah's child brain hears the explicit words "I love you." However, the physical abuse imprints an implicit message of "I don't love you because I don't care about your safety." The words and actions do not align. In fact, they contradict each other. From the mixed messages and abuse, Noah may internalize that his mother doesn't actually love him. Going a step further, he might also internalize that something is wrong with him because his mother treats him this way (that he must deserve the treatment for something he did).

> *Liza is fourteen and has a very close relationship with her mother. Liza's body is beginning to fill out differently, and Liza sees herself as larger than her peers. When Liza expresses to her mother that she feels self-conscious and uncomfortable with her body size, her mother tries to encourage her by telling her that size doesn't matter. However, Liza is confused because she has watched her mother count her own calories and weigh herself daily for several years. She has heard her mom describe herself as "fat" and "ugly" when looking in the mirror at herself.*

Liza, even at fourteen, is confused about what her mom really believes about size. She hears her mom's words, but doesn't believe her encouragement because she has observed a pattern to her mother's perception of body size and interpretation of what body size means to her mother.

When situations like these happen during childhood, brain development complicates matters because children don't yet have the mental capacity to decipher all the factors at play. In Noah's case, for example, he is too young to understand his mother loves him but has an alcohol addiction. Children often don't have the mental capacity to assign appropriate meaning to events, particularly when no one is clarifying or correcting what they infer from the information.

From an evolutionary survival standpoint, the brain analyzes implicit messages to assess situations and predict future danger. We need this information processing to occur. Imagine being in front of someone who directly says, "I am not going to hurt you," but they are pointing a gun toward you. Our system needs to understand the potential threat inferred by the gun.

The problem, as it relates to identity development and self-worth, is often we internalize the wrong meaning from implied messages. And these internalized implied messages often leave a much more powerful imprint on our understanding of ourselves and the world than explicit information. Consequently, we learn to behave in response to the meaning we assign to these messages, which we will explore further in the next chapter.

You have likely internalized messages from implied information throughout your life beginning in childhood. You are not bad or wrong for absorbing implied messages because, again, you are merely operating as all humans do. As a child, you did not have the capacity to make full sense of any situation, both because of your brain development stage and because people around you were not aware of the implied messages they were sending and, thus, the effects of their actions. The messages you took away from childhood around self-worth were not your fault. You did not have the capacity to know better or see life through a different lens.

Imperfection

Can you name anyone you know who is perfect?

Just one person?

If anyone comes to mind, then first please let me know who they are because I am intrigued and want to know more about them. Second, I challenge you to reflect: Are they perfect, or do you only see perfection? Are you blind to their flaws?

Living in the wide media world today, it can appear that some people might actually be perfect or darn close to it. That is because people only show what they want to show. Do they hop on and record a live video of when they are yelling at their partner or passive-aggressively answering their parent during a heated discussion? No, they do not. This public display of only good isn't new, however. It happened long before social media. Some people are really good at portraying themselves as having everything together, seamlessly juggling obligations, achieving every goal, having perfect relationships without discord—the list goes on. But they too struggle, even if behind closed doors. I know this to be true because perfection is not humanly possible. We are not built to know everything. If we do not know everything, we are bound to make mistakes. We are not built to be always emotionally regulated. We are designed to learn while navigating all that life brings our way.

Innocence

Right now, I invite you to think of a baby or a small child. If you have one yourself or know one, bring this tiny human to mind. Picture the way they sleep. Visualize the way they look into the eyes of the person holding them and feeding them. Picture them playing on the ground trying to make a toy fit together with something else. Imagine their crying when they are upset. Imagine their giggling and smiling when something makes them laugh. See their innocence. Notice how they came into this world having done *nothing* wrong. All they have done is come into this world needing someone to care for them so they can survive. They have entered the world automatically worthy of love, compassion, and connection.

Now, imagine you as this little human. Close your eyes, take a deep breath, and really take this in. I invite you to see your own innocence. You, too, were born into this world having done nothing wrong, being beautiful just as you are. You, too, were born innocent, relying on the outside world to take care of you. You were born worthy of love, worthy of compassion, and worthy of connection.

Every part of you that developed after your innocent arrival into the world was in direct response to the environment around you. After your birth, other people and events started shaping you. You watched. You copied. You tried different things. Some of your behaviors and traits were positively reinforced. Others were negatively reinforced. And most of your development came to be before your brain was fully developed and before you were conscious of what was going on. The majority of how you act and think today was built on your childhood foundational experiences and circumstances. Life events might have clouded your understanding or judgment to steer you away from seeing and knowing this innocence. But that doesn't mean your innocence and limitless worth disappeared. They just got hidden behind the messy human experience.

Personal Reflection

What is it like to get in touch with your innocence? Can you visualize your younger self? Can you pinpoint when you lost sight of the innocent, perfectly imperfect child you were? How do you feel when you think about this? How would you like to get back to honoring your innocence?

Self-Judgment and Self-Compassion

The Merriam-Webster Dictionary defines compassion as "sympathetic consciousness of others' distress with a desire to alleviate it." Imagine seeing a young boy sitting on the side of a playground with his head buried in his knees and crying. You immediately wonder what is wrong and if he is okay. Or imagine you are sitting in an airport and the person next to you, who is on the phone, starts crying and hyperventilating. They exclaim, "Oh, my God!" repeatedly as tears stream down their face. Often the natural instinct is to wonder what their pain is about and feel bad for their pain and want to console them. This is compassion for others.

Self-compassion is having that same genuine concern and care for *yourself*. Essentially, it is being kind to yourself as you would be to someone else. Self-compassion is a term that is becoming more and more common, yet many are not completely clear what it means or what it looks like on a practical level. Self-compassion includes kindness to self, acceptance of mistakes or shortcomings, understanding, curiosity, and forgiveness. It is the process of moving beyond judgment and toward embracing all of yourself and your humanity.

Because you are reading this book to improve your sense of worth, I can almost guarantee you lack compassion for yourself. Instead, you judge yourself and hold yourself to unrealistic standards. Judgment means to assign value to something as good or bad. Self-judgment is the process of putting yourself down because you have determined that something is bad about you or about what you have done. This comes from expecting too much from yourself. You set standards based on where you think you should be rather than where you are. You compare yourself to others without having all the facts. Your self-worth takes hits every day because of how you mentally treat yourself in response to your judgment that something is wrong with you. Overall, you treat yourself worse than you treat others because you lose sight that you are just as deserving of understanding, empathy, and kindness.

Imagine a six-year-old kid comes to you and says, "That person over there is being mean to me. They won't let me play with them. They said it's because they don't like my glasses." What would your most natural response be? Would it sound like, "Well, your glasses make you ugly, so it makes sense." Absolutely not, right? That would be incredibly hurtful. Instead, you might give them a hug and say something like, "You are amazing. Your glasses are a great part of you and your look," or "I am sorry they are leaving you out. I imagine that hurts your heart." Having self-compassion is learning to treat yourself the way you would that six-year-old.

One of the best things you can do for yourself is learn self-compassion. Self-compassion includes:

- Learning about yourself through a lens of nonjudgmental (neutral) curiosity.
- Meeting yourself where you are today, in this moment.
- Validating your emotions and thoughts.
- Creating room for grace and forgiveness.
- Normalizing making mistakes and imperfection.
- Speaking to yourself using loving, supportive language.

Nurturing yourself with kindness and understanding is possibly the most important thing you could ever do for yourself. And I know how hard it can be to learn self-compassion. It takes time to recondition the patterns of how you treat yourself. When you recognize you are being hard on yourself but finding it difficult to turn it around, flip your situation and imagine someone you love going through the same thing. Imagine what you would say and do to show love and compassion. Then write these ideas down as statements to yourself. If you hear a voice that rationalizes, "But I don't deserve the same understanding," remind yourself that you are an equally innocent human who is deserving of love.

Personal Forgiveness

One of the gifts of being human is the ability to reflect on past situations to learn to do them differently in the future. This process allows us to grow and evolve. At the same time, if you are too harsh on yourself for your previous actions and past versions of yourself, you are unfairly not allowing yourself to experience compassion for your present self.

One of the biggest traps people fall into (as I, too, have done) is to compare your past self with your current tools and maturity. Remember that your past was based on an older version of you who did not know what you know today. So, give that younger and less experienced version of yourself compassionate forgiveness. Honor what it was going through at the time and what it did not yet know. You can provide forgiveness to yourself *and* be committed to trying to upgrade your knowledge and tools each day moving forward.

Embracing Your Humanity

Combining everything from this chapter, below you can read through common examples of thoughts people express when they have unfair or unrealistic expectations of themselves. In the second column, you will read new ways of seeing yourself that support extending compassion for your humanity. Use this chart to explore how to remind yourself that you are human.

Unfair/Unrealistic Expectations	Extending Compassion for Your Humanity
I should have known better.	I responded based on what I knew at the time. I didn't have the information to know differently.
I should have controlled my emotions.	My brain detected danger and responded accordingly.
I know better.	I know better in theory, but I have not developed the skill to act accordingly.
I shouldn't still be grieving.	Emotions take time to process. The body needs effective outlets to process emotions. Emotions cannot just be turned off.
I am such a failure for freezing in front of the crowd when it was time to give my speech.	My body went into a stress response. I am learning to calm my nervous system.
I am a horrible person for being such a bully to others in middle school.	My brain was not fully developed so I made decisions I wouldn't make today.
I can't believe I am crying about this so many years later. I am so weak.	My body has been holding on to this trauma for so long without processing it. Crying is the body's natural way of releasing energy, stress, and emotions.
I shouldn't have made that mistake.	We make mistakes.
In my mind I know it isn't true, so I shouldn't feel this way.	It takes time and experience for our logical brain and emotions to align.
I should have known how to do it.	You can't know something you have never been taught.
No one else has these struggles.	It seems like others don't have this problem, but realistically they probably just don't show it or talk about it.

Embracing Your Human Journey

It is natural and normal for us to lose sight of how we are designed to function as humans. We can get caught up in the cultural expectations to be superheroes devoid of emotions, setbacks, and challenges. We can return to buying into the stories that perfection is possible and that comparing ourselves to others is the best way to determine our worth. But the way to embody your worth is to honor and nurture your personal journey as a human living in this complicated world. Learning to have compassion and understanding for how you function widens the possibility for you to truly love yourself and discover your immeasurable worth. Consequently, the more compassion you cultivate for yourself, the more you can extend love to and connect with others.

In the next chapter, you will build on the concepts from this chapter by gaining a deeper understanding of how you came to be. You will be able to identify how you learned to survive thus far. This will help you deepen your compassion for your life journey up to this point. From there, you will be able to explore and modify your strategies as you see fit, which will lead you to improving your techniques for getting through life.

Personal Reflection

1. Which concepts from this chapter help you understand yourself better and why?
2. On a scale of zero (I don't give myself compassion at all) to ten (I am always compassionate toward myself), how do you rate yourself overall?
3. When is it easier to have compassion for yourself? What makes it easier?
4. When is self-criticism and judgment more present/harder to quiet? Why is it harder to give yourself grace, love, or understanding in these situations?
5. When are you able to extend compassion for others but not yourself? What is the difference?
6. How can embracing your humanity help you feel more love and compassion toward yourself?

CHAPTER 2
Understanding Survival Strategies

"I understand now that I am not a mess
but a deeply feeling person in a messy world."
— Glennon Doyle

As complicated people living in a messy world, each one of us is bound to experience challenging life events or circumstances. When these challenges occur during childhood, we begin to develop what I call "survival strategies." Survival strategies are the conscious and unconscious behavioral patterns we employ to cope with life. They are more complicated and intricate than going for a run when stressed or having a drink of alcohol to numb emotions. They always exist to keep us safe and alive. These survival strategies eventually become so reinforced that they essentially become part of one's personality or everyday manner of existing.

The Origin of My Survival Strategies

My mom and biological father, Lee, divorced when I was two. We had all been living together in Denver, Colorado, but when my parents separated, my mom and I moved to Idaho to be near her family. My contact with Lee was limited once we moved to Idaho, so I distinctly remember the first time I got to see him after we had moved. I was almost five at the time, and I was so incredibly excited to see him! I had really missed him.

Much to my and my mom's surprise, when we met up with Lee, he had an unknown woman with him. After he and I hugged, he introduced me to her…and excitedly told me she was his new girlfriend.

And then he proceeded to tell me they were expecting a baby.

I was devastated.

I remember my heart-broken confusion. I didn't understand how he could leave us and choose to be with someone else. I could not wrap my mind around him being excited to have another child but not wanting to be in my life more.

This was the beginning of me feeling not good enough. I couldn't help but wonder if I had done something wrong that made him not want to be a part of my life but eager to raise someone else.

He had that baby, my half-sister, soon after our visit, and then he had my half-brother two years later.

Fast forward to seventeen. At this point, my mom and I were living in Colorado again with my dad, Bob, and Lee was living in Albuquerque, New Mexico. Lee drove up one weekend in the spring of 1996 to see me. I had not seen him in three years. And between the two visits, I rarely heard from him. I was again excited to see him, but I also felt nervous because it had been so long since we had visited in person.

On our last evening of the three days together, as he drove me back to my house from dinner, he spent the entire ride talking about how he needed to be a good father to my half-sister and half-brother. At that point, he was raising them on his own because he had divorced their mother, and she lived in another state. We arrived at my house and said our goodbyes. I knew it would likely be a long time until I saw him again, so part of me was sad and reluctant to say goodbye. At the same time, once we hugged goodbye, I closed the front door behind me, turned to my mom, and proceeded to cry like a baby in her arms. "Why does he want to do what is best for them but not for me?" I asked her between sobs. I felt this complete sense of despair and confusion—how was I not good enough to get the same dedication and commitment from him? My undeveloped mind was convinced I must have done something wrong. I wasn't capable (no matter how many times other people told me otherwise) of understanding his absence was about him, not about something being wrong with me. I could not comprehend that someone could love you *and* not be there for you. I did not understand why I was not good enough compared to my half-siblings.

Growing up, my mom and dad (Bob) were really strict. I hated getting in trouble and became really dysregulated when I did something wrong because I hated disappointing them. I was terrified I could make such a big mistake one day that would cause them to stop loving me or abandon me. They could tell me a million times that was not going to happen, but my internal system did not believe it because of my experience with Lee. I figured if one parent could leave, then any parent (or person) could leave.

In response to my internal misunderstanding that I caused Lee to abandon me and the belief that others could just as easily leave, I tried to do everything perfectly. I set out to constantly prove I was "good enough." I consistently earned straight As. I signed up for leadership positions in the clubs I joined. I avoided getting in any kind of trouble at home. I apologized for anything and everything, taking responsibility for any imperfection I displayed. A critic developed inside me to judge and assess everything I did so I could figure out how to do it better. If I could identify how to do things well or how to do them better, I could make the appropriate changes to minimize my future risk of making mistakes. Ultimately, I was just trying to prevent the loss and pain that could arise as a result of my imperfections.

I also learned to motivate myself by criticizing my work. I was constantly assessing my efforts as not good enough; I needed to "do better." I pushed myself to always aim higher. But this made life very stressful. It was impossible to maintain the effort of my perfectionism. This was one of the causes of my breakdown in my junior year of college. I couldn't perform to my own unrealistic standards anymore.

As I began to understand these behaviors as survival strategies, I began to gain awareness of my underlying intentions and needs. This allowed me to develop alternative strategies to meet my needs in ways that worked better for me. I now find strategies that support my self-worth and well-being rather than seeking someone else's approval.

The Creation of Survival Strategies

Have you ever been perplexed by someone's behavior, but once you learned their "story," their behavior made sense to you? From learning their story, you felt more compassion and understanding about why they operate the way they do. For example, I know someone who works extremely hard, holding down multiple jobs. They are extremely frugal and prioritize saving money instead of spending it. They don't take vacations. They don't go to fancy places. At first, I didn't understand why they limited their spending so intensely, but when I learned they had experienced extreme poverty as a child, it made sense to me.

You learn survival strategies in different ways. One way is through direct learning, meaning someone explicitly teaches you how to do it. Telling a child to stop crying and stating "Strong people don't cry" is an example of learning a lesson from direct teaching. The subsequent lesson is you need to hold back emotion to be strong in life. And this lesson has supported many people in pushing forward through life.

The next way you learn is through implicit messages. Remember, implicit means indirect, vague, or ambiguous. These messages are learned indirectly without someone specifically spelling out how to do something. Imagine a child who watches their parents fight often. A parent may explicitly say, "This is Mommy and Daddy's problem. You don't need to worry about it." However, then imagine the child gets hurt one day while the mom and dad are fighting. The parents stop fighting and rush to the child to see what is wrong. The child may then implicitly learn, "If I can divert their attention, they will stop fighting." No one explicitly tells the child this, and the child is not explicitly saying this to themselves, but because the event interrupted their fighting, the child may start to create a pattern of diverting attention in this way. This then becomes an innocent strategy the child uses in future situations when the parents fight.

As you repeat these strategies, you begin to notice (consciously or not) when they benefit your safety or wellbeing in some way. You continue using them in different situations when you consciously or unconsciously believe they are, ultimately, protecting you.

The Good and Bad of Survival Strategies

All survival strategies initially serve a purpose in your life. You may not be aware of the purpose at first, but as you examine them, you will see how they try to support your wellbeing. Most often a strategy is an attempt to keep you safe or create the perception of safety. These strategies have good aspects. For example, my "perfection" strategy served me well in many ways. Namely, because I applied myself so diligently to my studies and extracurricular activities, I earned a full scholarship to one of the best undergraduate universities in the country. I consistently received praise for how well I did in school. This boosted my self-esteem and proved I could achieve my goals. Later, after my dad died, I used this strategy to keep moving toward my dreams, particularly career-wise.

And yet, survival strategies can have drawbacks. The strategies may include behaviors, thoughts, or emotions that eventually become counterproductive to your overall wellbeing. For me, the major drawback of my perfectionist survival strategy was I was striving for something I could never achieve: perfection. I held myself (and others) to impossible standards. When I fell short of these standards, my self-judgment came in full force. All I could think was, *See, you're just not good enough,* or *You're a fuckup because you can't even get this right.* I internalized these "imperfections" as further proof I was not good enough. Therefore, the exact strategy I was using to combat feeling not good enough led to critiquing myself harshly, with unreasonably high expectations, so the strategy eventually reinforced my feelings of inadequacy.

Examples of Survival Strategies

Let's walk through some scenarios that illustrate the presence of survival strategies. I invite you to read the following examples and then answer the reflection questions. As you read each example, think about how the person described is trying to cope and survive.

Savannah is a female in her early twenties. She grew up with two biological parents and a younger brother named Cole. When Savannah was a child, Cole endured multiple illnesses that led him to the hospital many times. On a few occasions, Cole was near death due to his medical issues. During Cole's hospital stays, Savannah had some level of understanding of how dire things were for her brother and, therefore, sensed the weight of the stress on her parents' shoulders. In response to the situation, she tried to be helpful any way she could. She also never wanted to add extra stress to the situation, so she learned to figure things out on her own and kept her problems private.

Fast forward to today. Savannah is struggling because she often overextends herself by helping others before taking care of herself. She does not tell others what she needs or what she is experiencing. Savannah internalized a belief that her needs are secondary to others. She internalized that it is "selfish" to ask for her needs to be met and sees her needs as "minor" or even "trivial" compared to those of others. No one said her needs didn't matter or she was selfish to ask for them to be met. This was just the result of the circumstances of her early life where a beloved family member's needs came first.

Scenario Reflection

1. What strategies did Savannah develop as a child?
2. How did Savannah's strategies help her get through tough times in her childhood?
3. How might these strategies protect her today?

4. How might these strategies be counterproductive for her well-being and self-worth today?
5. What alternative strategy could Savannah use today to move forward?

Julio is a twenty-three-year-old man. He was raised by his father, Carlos. One of Carlos' biggest strengths as a father was that he was a hard worker, working up to eighty hours a week, to provide for Julio and Julio's siblings. Carlos grew up poor and went through times of hunger and inability to pay the bills. As a result, Carlos developed a sense of responsibility for always having enough money in the bank to ensure their basic needs would never be threatened. At the same time, Carlos had strict expectations of Julio, particularly regarding doing well in school so Julio could build a successful career for himself later in life. Julio learned he was expected to stay focused on school and developed the appropriate skills to do so.

Carlos also parented with the mentality of "buck up" and "pull yourself up by your bootstraps." If Julio became upset as a child, his father would say, "There is no time for crying. Get back to focusing on your schoolwork." Carlos' survival strategy was to set aside emotion so he could focus on working and earning money to provide for his children. In turn, Julio learned to stifle his emotions because he was taught the way to survive is to block emotions and focus on productivity.

Last year, during Julio's senior year of college, his father, Carlos, suffered a fatal heart attack. While Julio experienced grief throughout the year, he played out the lessons he learned from his father: power through emotions and stay focused on school. Since then, Julio has lost forty pounds from loss of appetite, has little motivation to go to work or socialize, and has difficulty getting through the day without crying. He tells his best friend, "I should be over my dad's death" and asked, "Why can't I just get my shit together and move on?"

Scenario Reflection

1. What strategies did Carlos develop to survive?
2. How did Carlos' coping strategies help him get through life?
3. How did Julio's learned strategies benefit him?
4. How did these strategies become counterproductive to Julio's well-being and self-esteem today?

As a young child, Marcus was quiet and kind. Physically, he was almost always shorter than his peers. When he was in the second grade, he switched schools and didn't know anyone. At this school, he started getting bullied about his height. He became an easy target due to his quiet temperament because his peers knew he wouldn't speak up. The bullying included both verbal and physical acts. In fourth grade, a bully physically injured Marcus, giving him a concussion. School administrators were informed of the incident, but they did nothing to intervene and support Marcus. Marcus continued to endure bullying for the next few years.

In seventh grade, Marcus grew significantly and built a lot of physical strength through playing football. As a result, he started feeling more powerful. That led to him fighting back when bullied or pushed around. He started getting in physical fights regularly. As he began to "win" these fights, his peers started bothering him less. By eighth grade, peers warned others, "Don't mess with Marcus. He will take you down."

Since the school administrators did not set boundaries with the bullies, Marcus learned he needed to take matters into his own hands and defend himself. When he became stronger, his survival strategy was to become feared by others. Although his quiet and kind personality had not changed in the presence of safe and trusting people, these traits became secondary to survival in his mind. Whenever Marcus got suspended for fighting, he felt it was worth it because it was better than feeling dehumanized, powerless, and scared.

Scenario Reflection

1. What strategies did Marcus develop to get through tough times in his childhood?
2. How did these strategies help him?
3. How did these strategies become counterproductive for him?

Identifying Your Survival Strategies

On the next few pages, you will find a list of several common survival strategies. Each strategy is broken down into four sections. The first section names the type of strategy and the common behaviors associated with it. The next section describes the possible life circumstances that led to the development of the strategy. The third section names how the strategy feels protective or beneficial. The last section lists how the pattern may be counterproductive to your well-being or sense of worth.

As you review the list to identify the strategies you relate to, keep the following in mind:

1. Identify your age when you started using the strategy and reflect on the circumstances that led to using the strategy. Notice the innocence of your younger self when you came up with the strategy to try to protect your sense of safety and sense of worth.
2. Examine your strategies through a lens of curiosity and compassion. You are trying to learn about yourself without passing judgment.
3. Validate how the strategy served or continues to serve you.
4. Nonjudgmentally review how you would like to change the strategy if it no longer serves you overall.

I think it is important to mention that when most people are asked, "How has this strategy served you?" they immediately respond with, "It doesn't." This automatic response occurs either because we are aware of how the behaviors have negative consequences or because someone else has criticized us for the pattern. If this is your initial response, take a deep breath and return to curiosity without judgment.

Perfectionism

- You strive for perfection in nearly everything you do.
- You do not allow room for error.
- You set very high standards (often unrealistic) for yourself and/or others.
- You hold higher standards for yourself than you hold for others.
- You believe you need to always meet others' expectations.

Possible Causes

- You experienced harsh (up to abusive) consequences when you made mistakes.
- Your behaviors or traits were often scrutinized or shamed.
- You experienced an event (or events) that had a tragic outcome (i.e., fatal car accident).
- You craved the approval of someone because they did not demonstrate consistent or unconditional love.
- You only got attention when you did things well.

Protective Outcomes

- The more you achieve or the better you perform, the more you minimize risk of negative outcomes.
- If you don't make mistakes, others cannot criticize you.
- When you meet your expectations, you feel more in control.
- You receive praise and attention for your accomplishments, giving you a temporary feeling of good enough.
- Your high expectations motivate you to do well and persevere.

Counterproductive Outcomes

- You cannot meet perfection standards, so you set yourself up to fall short of expectations.
- When you or others don't meet your expectations, you feel disappointment.
- Your feelings of accomplishment are outweighed by feelings of failure or not good enough.
- You become exhausted from trying to meet such high expectations all the time.
- You limit your ability to embrace your imperfections and see them as unique strengths.

People Pleasing

- You do things for others to make them happy or gain their approval.
- You prioritize others' wants and needs above your own.
- You hide yourself by not voicing your personality and preferences.
- You abandon your own wants and needs.
- You aim to never rock the boat.

Possible Causes

- Your safety and security depended on your taking care of someone else above yourself.
- You were not given guidance on how to get your needs met.
- Your wants and needs were ignored, denied, or scrutinized.
- Adults in your life modeled and advocated for you to put your needs second to others.

Protective Outcomes

- You keep others happy or satisfied.

- You minimize the potential for others to get mad at you.
- You feel safer when you know others' needs are met.
- You receive praise or acknowledgment for being so kind and selfless.

Counterproductive Outcomes

- Your wants and needs get neglected.
- You don't stand up for yourself when it is beneficial to your well-being.
- Others get so used to you not expressing your wants that they neglect to ask you.
- You develop feelings of resentment for your wants and needs not being met.
- You feel unimportant.

Keeping Busy/Overworking/Overextension

- You dedicate significant resources to school, work, or projects.
- You apply extended time to school, work, or projects.
- You neglect taking time for important things outside of your chosen focus.
- You do not leave room for rest or self-care.
- You over commit yourself and wear yourself out.

Possible Causes

- You were taught achievement and success are the keys to life.
- You discovered if you focus attention on tasks or achievements, you can avoid stresses from other areas in your life.
- You were praised for your achievements, dedication, and hard work.

- You only received attention when you achieved something.

Protective Outcomes

- You feel an increased sense of pride, thus self-worth, by achieving things.
- You feel a sense of purpose.
- You decrease your feelings of failure.
- You feel more in control of your life because of what you do.
- You benefit from the increased resources that come as a result of your achievements and hard work (such as higher salary or job promotions).

Counterproductive Outcomes

- You attach your self-worth to what you do or produce, so your self-esteem becomes contingent on external factors.
- Your life feels overwhelming, exhausting, or unbalanced.
- Over time, you lose passion and motivation for the activity.
- You feel inadequate or worthless in other areas that you are neglecting.
- You neglect other areas of your life such as self-care or relationships.
- You avoid working through difficult things in your life that need your attention.

Overthinking/Ruminating

- You prioritize thinking over feeling.
- You analyze situations from every angle possible.
- You replay past situations over and over again to find out where things went off course or could have gone differently.

- You imagine future situations and play out various scenarios in your mind to plan for any possible situation.

Possible Causes

- You were taught that thinking through things is the most reliable resource you have.
- You had to meticulously read other people's actions or behaviors to predict their potentially unsafe responses.
- You were questioned for behaviors your displayed or emotions you had and, therefore, had to justify yourself.
- You were encouraged to use your analytical skills and discouraged to have an emotional response.

Protective Outcomes

- You can break things down into multiple steps.
- You can foresee potential problems in future scenarios and plan accordingly.
- You can anticipate negative reactions from others and plan accordingly.
- You can plan ahead to maximize probable positive outcomes.
- You can identify and learn from past missteps by reviewing what went wrong.
- Your thinking ahead provides a sense of control and relief.

Counterproductive Outcomes

- You excessively worry about things that cannot be accurately predicted or controlled.
- Your thinking distracts from internal emotional processing and releasing of energy.

- You sometimes incorrectly predict problems or incorrectly "mind read" what someone else is thinking, causing you more stress.
- Your body feels constant anxiety in response to your worrisome thoughts.
- You have difficulty embracing the present moment and recognizing that you are okay in the here-and-now.
- You become overly frustrated when you can't resolve your emotions through thought.

Chronic Incompletion

- You struggle to finish tasks and projects.
- You do things only part way before you give up.
- You start new projects and goals before you finish the current one.
- You keep chasing the next best thing.

Possible Causes

- High expectations were placed on you to keep accomplishing things.
- You perceive that you have failed in the past so will fail again.
- You took risks in the past that did not meet your expectations.
- You were told that what you were doing was not good enough so you went on to the next thing.

Protective Outcomes

- If you don't finish something, then the end result cannot be judged.
- You avoid failure or disappointment if you never actually finish something.
- You keep yourself busy and moving.

Counterproductive Outcomes

- You do not give yourself a chance to succeed.
- You end up never feeling a sense of accomplishment or pride.
- You feel an underlying sense of failure because of never finishing things.

Self-Judgment

- You are constantly overly critical of yourself.
- You put yourself down with name calling and labeling.
- You blame yourself for things that are not blame-worthy.
- You beat yourself up for perceived mistakes.

Possible Causes

- You had overly critical caregivers who used the same critical language.
- You have been shamed by others.
- Your caregivers had exceedingly high expectations of you.
- You discovered it was safer to judge yourself than those who were harming you.

Protective Outcomes

- You are always on guard to detect your mistakes or shortcomings before others can criticize you.
- You can pinpoint your faults or mistakes and then course correct.
- You keep yourself from becoming arrogant or superior to others.

Counterproductive Outcomes

- You train yourself to see only your faults.

- You blind yourself from your strengths.
- You feel awful about yourself because of your constant put-downs.
- You reject praise and don't accept or believe compliments from others.
- Others stop complimenting you because they know you will reject their compliments.
- You treat yourself worse than you treat others.
- You have too harsh of expectations for yourself.

Over-Responsibility/Over-Control

- You take on responsibility that belongs to others.
- You take on blame that should be attributed to others.
- You overextend yourself because you are taking on more than what belongs on your plate.
- You don't give others a chance to do things because you believe you can do them better.
- You don't accept help from others.

Possible Causes

- You couldn't rely on others to take care of their own responsibilities.
- Your caregivers weren't capable or available to take care of adult tasks so you had to fill in for them.
- Your caregivers delegated over-responsibility to you (often tied to your sibling order or gender).
- You were expected to act as a parent in some capacity so became parentified.

- You felt like you were the only one capable of protecting others and had evidence to prove it.

Protective Outcomes

- You control the outcomes by taking over.
- You ensure an increased probability of positive results because it is done right or thoroughly.
- You can predictably influence other people's emotions and actions by taking control of the situation first.
- You feel good when you take care of others.

Counterproductive Outcomes

- You prevent others from taking care of themselves.
- You inhibit others from meeting your needs or wants because you beat them to it.
- You feel overwhelmed because your needs get neglected.
- You feel alone and unimportant when others don't reciprocate an equal responsibility or concern.

Hide/Avoid Feelings

- You push your emotions down and pretend as though they don't exist.
- You compartmentalize your emotions by focusing on other things.

Possible Causes

- You had no role models on how to process emotions.
- Your caregivers modeled avoiding feelings.
- Your emotions were often dismissed or ridiculed.

- You experienced negative consequences for showing emotion.
- Your emotional expression was used against you.
- You went through something emotionally powerful but were told not to cry about it and/or to just move on.

Protective Outcomes

- You have developed strong thinking skills.
- You have the ability to compartmentalize, which is beneficial in some circumstances.
- You are able to stay focused or calm during emotionally activating situations.
- You are perceived as strong.

Counterproductive Outcomes

- You have difficulty feeling and processing emotions.
- Your body experiences physical symptoms tied to the unprocessed emotions (to which you may even be unaware they are connected).
- You experience decreased connection to others.

Personal Reflection

Reviewing the examples above (and any others you thought of that aren't on the list), reflect on the following:

1. Which strategies do you relate to and why?
2. How did these strategies innocently develop?
3. How did these strategies help you earlier in your life? (How did they keep you safe or help you feel better about yourself?)
4. What is the underlying goal of each strategy?
5. How do they continue to serve you today?

6. How are they counterproductive to your goals or wellbeing today?
7. How do they help your sense of worth?
8. How do they lower your sense of worth or ability to embody your worth?
9. Do you still need or want to use the same strategies moving forward? Why or why not?
10. Are there other patterns that are not on this list that you can explore using the same format and questions?

Growth Activity

Write a letter to your younger self during a challenging time when you were just trying to learn how to cope with life. If it helps you to get in touch with this younger version of yourself, you can look at a picture of yourself or a picture of another kid (imagining they were going through what you went through). For some people, this can be an emotionally difficult task. If you do not feel you are ready (if some part of you says "no"), then I welcome you to honor that "no." You can always come back to this activity later when you feel ready. If you do choose to write the letter, include the following elements.

1. Acknowledge the innocence in how you developed your strategies. This might sound like, "You had limited support in learning how to cope with your emotions, so you did the best you could."
2. Show compassion for what little you went through. This might sound like, "I see how hard it was for you. I see how painful it was for you to lose someone at such a young age."
3. Express gratitude for the strategies your younger self came up with. This might sound like, "Thank you for being so well-behaved. You saved us from getting hit."
4. Express praise for resilience and creativity. This might sound like, "Holy cow! You were one smart cookie to figure out how to predict someone's emotions and actions."

5. Notice anywhere in your body that you can feel a positive sensation associated with the validation and understanding you are giving your younger self. Be with the sensation and breathe into it, allowing it to be present.

Bonus Growth Activity

Write a letter to your current self about a current strategy you use. Follow the same steps as the letter to your younger self. Do this whenever you notice yourself judging the way you operate, so you can practice feeling love and appreciation toward the innocent desire and strategy.

Assess and Realign Your Strategies

I can't say this enough: The strategies that began years ago served a purpose. At the same time, as we get older and move through life's stages, we may not need them the same way we needed them before. For example, I no longer need to overextend myself by making sure everything I do is done to my best ability. In high school, this served me well because it helped me get into my dream college. Today, however, my achievements and timelines are solely defined by me. I have the latitude to define which activities are worth putting 100 percent effort into and which activities I want to dedicate less effort and energy toward.

When exploring the survival strategies, if you determine parts or all of the strategy do not quite meet your present needs or you discover they keep you from feeling good about yourself or growing, you can explore other strategies that might serve you better.

To make adjustments:

1. Identify the underlying goal of the strategy. (What is the strategy trying to help with?) Examples of underlying goals might include:
    - Minimizing risk of harm
    - Being prepared for potential challenges
    - Feeling loved

2. List the ways the strategy helps meet the underlying goal.
3. List the ways the strategy doesn't achieve the underlying goal.
4. Brainstorm alternative behaviors that can help you achieve the underlying goal.

Honoring the Survival Strategies of Others

All too often we take other people's behavior personally, thinking their behaviors reflect how they feel about us. For example, I used to be convinced if certain people really cared about me, they would act a certain way to display that love. So, if they did not act in certain "loving" ways, I assumed it meant they didn't truly love me. I had the same thought process with Lee. I thought, *If he really loved me, he would stay in contact with me.*

I am so thankful I see his behavior differently now. I realized his withdrawal was merely a survival strategy. When he felt like a failure (which I imagine he felt often, knowing him), he withdrew. In the last letter he wrote to me, he said, "It seems I take one step forward and two steps back, and it is really starting to get to me.... I don't mean to share all this bad news, but I owed you an explanation." In my young mind, I preferred for him to communicate with me, so I was okay with hearing things weren't going well. Based on what I know now, he may have felt so guilty about his depression and how he managed it that he withdrew to protect me from feeling burdened and protect himself from feeling like a bad father. It is not that he didn't love me. It's that he didn't know how to do better. He was going through his own struggles, and his way of coping was to back away. When I read his letters now, his depth of love for me is so clear. *And* he was surviving the best he knew how.

When you can recognize other people's attempts to cope, it helps you see most of other people's behavior is not about you or a reflection of how they feel about you. When you can see someone just innocently acting to create safety, often from an automatic conditioned response because they don't know how to do it differently, life feels more peaceful. This, therefore, opens the door for deeper connection with others.

Personal Reflection

Identify someone whose survival strategies you want to get more curious about. This could be someone in your life currently or someone from your past.

1. Which strategy(ies) do/did you see them employ?
2. If you know anything about their life history, how might they have needed these strategies to feel or be safe?
3. What do you know about their current situation that might prompt them to use these strategies?
4. What might you not know about them that could contribute to these strategies? (Example: They may be under financial stress or a close relative may be sick.)
5. If you chose an influential adult from your childhood, do you think they did the best they could with what they had or knew at the time?

A Lifetime Journey of Refinement

About six months after my son Ashton passed, I was back in the swing of things with a full private practice. Then I decided I was going to start writing this book, so I joined a book coaching program. I also decided to join a life coaching certification program to expand my business. One day, my mom said, "So it looks like you are doing that thing you do. You are overextending yourself to keep yourself busy." I laughed and said, "Nah, I genuinely feel called to do these things, and the book and coaching will overlap nicely. It won't be too much." She said, "Okay," with a laugh, which I knew was both humor and skepticism.

About six months later, I realized she was spot-on, seeing one of my survival strategies in action. She saw my pattern when I didn't. At that point, I recognized the innocence in my unconscious strategy showing up to help me cope with losing my son. When I became aware, I laughed too. I didn't judge myself. I honored the idea that focusing on projects was the best way I knew to feel a sense of hope and purpose so I could keep going amid a situation that could potentially strip me of all sense of hope and purpose. Since then, I have been playing around with how to balance the parts of this survival strategy that work for me and to modify the parts that don't.

Your default survival strategies will show up throughout your lifetime because they are the way you know how to operate. This is completely normal. It is not bad and does not need to be criticized. Once you recognize the pattern is showing up, you can consciously decide if it is the survival strategy you want to use or decide if you want to modify it in some way to ensure it helps you achieve your deepest desire. You will learn more and more ways to tweak your strategies so they work in your favor. You will be able to see patterns ahead of time and prepare. As a result, overall, you will be able to take better care of yourself and live more in alignment with behaviors that honor your worth.

In the next chapter, you will learn the powerful strategy of modifying your thoughts so they support the modifications you make to your survival strategies. You will learn to teach your mind to work in favor of your truth of being worthy. You will learn how to battle those thoughts that want to put you down or convince you that you are anything less than valuable.

CHAPTER 3
Repatterning Your Self-Talk

"I learned a long time ago, the wisest thing I can do is be on my own side."
— Maya Angelou

About two years into my relationship with Kevin, I looked over at him as he was lying on the couch staring at the ceiling. I was curious about what he was thinking because he appeared to be deep in thought. I asked him, "What are you thinking about right now?" He said, "Nothing." I had asked many times before and received the same answer. All of a sudden, a light bulb went off in my mind: He quite possibly could be not thinking of anything. This seemed unfathomable to me because my mind never seems to turn off.

After this fascinating realization, I questioned several people about their internal thought processes. I learned they all had some sort of internal dialogue going throughout the day, but that some people have constant internal chatter, and some people can quiet the noise. I did some research and learned it is perfectly normal to talk to yourself. In fact, some resources claim there are actual benefits to talking to yourself such as being able to think about something more objectively.[1]

However, *how* you talk to yourself matters. Your "self-talk," as it will be referred to in the rest of this book, directly influences the way you see yourself and how you experience your self-worth. The more you talk to

---

1 https://www.nytimes.com/2017/06/08/smarter-living/benefits-of-talking-to-yourself-self-talk.html. Accessed March 11, 2023.

yourself in a certain way (either positively or negatively), the more you believe what you are saying.

My Internal Dialogue

Writing has always been part of my life. From my preteens to early thirties, I often wrote in journals to process my thoughts and feelings. Therefore, in a way, this book has been in the works for years. In fact, in my early twenties, I often thought about writing a book about what I had been through. However, if I had written an autobiography back then based on how I viewed myself, it would have had an extremely different tone than this book. The content would have been very dark.

An apt title of that book would have been *Amanda, the Worthless Piece of Shit*. Chapters would have included:

Chapter One: Amanda Is Oversensitive and Cries Too Much

Chapter Two: Amanda Cares Too Much

Chapter Three: Amanda Is Not Good Enough

Chapter Four: Amanda Deserves Bad Things

If pages from my journals would have been included, you would read entries like these:

September 23, 1995:

What the hell is wrong with me? I'm such a fuckup. I can't believe I messed up like that in the routine tonight. I am sure I looked so stupid, and everyone noticed. And I'm sure some people think I don't deserve to have made the squad.

January 12, 1998:

Seriously, how could you be so stupid again to get your hopes up? Why would you ever think that you would get accepted into a sorority? Of course, you weren't picked by anyone. You looked like an idiot at each house, standing there barely knowing how to talk to anyone. Why can't you just be normal?

April 5, 2005:

> You're such an idiot. How could you have kidded yourself to think Dillon would actually like you? Once again, it is clear you aren't good enough. Just accept the fact that you will be alone forever. Seriously! There will always be someone who is better than you.

These are not actual journal entries because I shredded all of my journals when I packed up to move to Texas almost ten years ago. I no longer wanted to have the painful memories in my space. But the above statements are an authentic representation of what my journal entries said.

I am going to guess that my parents, roommates, and friends never read my journals, because if they had, they would have become aware of my very dark inner world. They would have been shocked at the number of extreme thoughts and how disparaging I was to myself. I would have further shocked people with the "evidence" I gathered to prove I was a worthless person.

I spent my twenties learning about the power and influence of thought. I began shifting the lens through which I saw myself by carefully modifying the way I talked to myself. This was an essential part of my journey toward self-love and appreciation.

Now my life story is titled *I Am Beyond Worthy*. I know I am valuable, beautiful, and have a purpose. And I treat myself as such in the privacy of my own mind.

Human Thought

A recent study estimates that humans have more than 6,000 thoughts per day.[2] That is a significant number! How many of those thoughts, however, are we actually conscious of? I know when we are speaking or writing,

2 "Brain meta-state transitions demarcate thoughts across task contexts exposing the mental noise of trait neuroticism," Nature.com, and "Discovery of 'thought worms' opens window to the mind," Medicalxpress.com. Both accessed March 9, 2023.

we are more conscious and deliberate with our thoughts. Think of when you need to send an important email. You sort your thoughts to decide which to include and how to specifically phrase your thoughts. At the same time, in many more moments we are significantly less conscious of our thoughts, particularly while doing activities we have done hundreds of times. Driving is a perfect example. Think of driving home from work and the number of times you don't fully remember all the individual moves you made. Yet you got home. And you most likely were thinking of other things simultaneously as your brain was processing the route home.

Many of our thoughts are fleeting, and we don't put too much emphasis on them. For example, think of the last time you walked into a store. You probably passed a sign on the way in. If you saw it with your eyes, your mind probably produced a thought acknowledging it. However, it was likely so fleeting you don't even remember seeing anything. But if you saw the sign every time you walked into the store, you would probably take more note of it because repetition and reinforcement heighten awareness.

Therefore, the number of times we have favorable or disparaging thoughts about ourselves or the world matters. If of the 6,000 thoughts we have a day, 80 percent are negative and focused on how bad of a person we are, this leads not just to having the thoughts but believing the thoughts.

Cognitive Bias

No one explicitly told me I was worthless or unimportant. In fact, people constantly told me they cared about me, praised my strengths, and contradicted me when I said negative things about myself. However, my self-perception was so low that what they said made little difference. If I did take in someone's feedback and allow myself to believe what they said, it most often provided momentary happiness, calm, or pride. It was just a matter of time (ten minutes, an hour, or a day) until I would encounter more "proof" I was not good enough, not important, or defective. That is because I did what all people do: I experienced the world through a biased lens. It's as if I wore a pair of glasses that only saw my imperfections and shortcomings.

As humans, we are designed to evaluate the world through biased lenses. In the psychology world, this is known as cognitive bias, which is the process in which "human cognition reliably produces representations that are systematically distorted compared to some aspect of objective reality."[3] Cognitive bias is said to be an evolutionary adaptation to assist humans in problem solving, making quick decisions, and detecting danger. This works well in a situation like being biased against hissing snakes. Hearing a hissing noise that sounds like a snake alerts most of us to move away from the snake so we don't get bitten.

However, filtering information to support the biased negative views we have of ourselves doesn't do us any good. We are inherently born worthy, so to filter information through a negative lens damages our well-being.

Thoughts Influence Emotions

When I ask people whether thoughts or emotions come first, most say emotions come before thoughts. This can certainly seem true, particularly when our emotions show up rapidly and intensely. However, the truth is emotions are based on thoughts.

Here is an example: Think of the times you have been in a checkout line at a store. If you are in the line and the person in front of you is having trouble with their credit card, you could have various thoughts. You could think, *Oh, man, I hate it when my card gets declined. I've had that happen for no reason before.* Emotionally, you may then feel relaxed and empathetic. In contrast, imagine you are running late. You think, *Ugh, I wish this person would go faster. I don't have time for this. I need to pick up my child in eight minutes. I can't be late because she will freak out.* It makes

3 Haselton, M. G. et al. "The Evolution of Cognitive Bias." In *The Handbook of Evolutionary Psychology*. Ed. D. M. Buss. Hoboken, NJ: John Wiley & Sons, 2005. p. 724–746.

sense that the subsequent emotions may include anxiety, frustration, and impatience.

It's important to recognize this relationship because it is common to identify your emotions before your thoughts. It is just kind of how we are trained. But if you can recognize that when you feel an emotion, it is the result of your thoughts, you can then work backward to try to figure out what you are experiencing. The rest of this chapter will teach you how to modify your thoughts, which will inevitably shift your emotional responses.

Cognitive Behavioral Therapy

When my mental health took its greatest nosedive from my posttraumatic breakdown in 1999, my parents found a psychologist for me to see a few times a week. His name was Dr. Edwards. He was probably in his sixties and seemed to have no personality at first because he rarely changed his expression or tone. My initial judgment of him was he was a stereotypical psychologist we would see in the movies. Because of this, I initially remember thinking, *How is this man going to help me?*

Dr. Edwards turned out to be a phenomenal therapist. In a way, he ended up being a godsend because he helped me stop feeling like I should end my life and taught me skills to take control. I know part of this success was due to his inclusion of cognitive therapy and his directive to use *The Feeling Good Handbook* by Dr. David Burns outside of sessions.

All therapists receive training in multiple treatment models. Each treatment model is based on a theory of why people do what they do, how people change, and techniques to facilitate this change. Because of my experience with Dr. Edwards, *The Feeling Good Handbook*, and my next phenomenal therapist, Jaime Calle, who also integrated cognitive therapy, I am a firm believer that cognitive therapy has value in the growth process toward embodying self-worth. Therefore, I feel it is imperative to include some of the concepts in this book.

Cognitive therapy was created by Dr. Aaron Beck who "contends that people with emotional difficulties tend to commit characteristic 'logical errors' that tilt objective reality in the direction of self-deprecation."[4] Beck coined the term "automatic thoughts."[5] In *The Feeling Good Handbook*, Dr. David Burns uses the terms "distortions" and "twisted thinking" to identify the processing errors that lead to incorrect or distorted views of self, others, and the world.[6] Other terms used synonymously with cognitive distortions include automatic negative thoughts (ANTS), limiting beliefs, thinking traps, or thinking errors. I most often refer to cognitive distortions as thinking errors, so that is the term I will primarily use in this chapter.

Thought Modification and Reframing

Identifying and understanding your thoughts is one piece of the puzzle. Going a step further, learning to modify your thoughts to match the reality of all evidence (not just the evidence you see through your filter) is a process that can drastically shift how you see and experience yourself. Building from the premise of cognitive therapy, the rest of the chapter will teach you how to recognize and modify your thought patterns. Dr. Burns refers to this process as "reframing" in which "You view a problem in a different light so that you think about it as something positive and good."[7] As we proceed through the rest of the chapter, I will use the term "thought modification" to refer to reframed thoughts and modified self-talk.

4 Corey, Gerald. *Theories and Techniques of Counseling.* Belmont, CA: Brooks/Cole, 2005. p. 284.

5 https://www.cbtcognitivebehavioraltherapy.com/aaron-beck-founder-of-cbt/. Accessed March 9, 2023.

6 *The Feeling Good Handbook.* New, York, NY: Plume, 1990.

7 *The Feeling Good Handbook.* p. 317.

Burns outlines ten cognitive distortion patterns. I am going to focus on the six that I know, when shifted, effectively realign your self-talk and experience of yourself. I will use a specific format to help you gain a solid understanding of thought patterns that contribute to negative self-beliefs and stories. I will also outline useful techniques to modify your thoughts. The format will include:

Thinking Error Type: This is the type of thinking error as categorized by *cognitive behavioral theorists.* Knowing the type of thought can be helpful for recognizing the characteristics and finding ways to alter the thought.

Burns Definition: This is the original definition of the cognitive distortion as defined by Dr. David Burns.

Description: This will describe what this thought type means and why it is detrimental to self-worth.

Examples: A list of examples will be provided of what this type of thought sounds like on a practical basis.

Buzzword(s): Buzzword is the term I use to reference the words you will hear that alert you to a possible thinking error. At first, it is going to be hard to hear your thinking errors. However, if you know the buzzword(s), then you will know to alert yourself to examine the validity of the thought.

Modification Technique(s) and Reframes: I will provide suggestions on how to reframe or modify the thought to be true to what you believe, think, or feel, and create a new thought based on accurate evidence. I find this aspect of many cognitive therapy resources lacking because people say, "I see how it is a negative thought, but how do I change it?" When you can reframe or modify the thought, you can shift the storyline completely.

Scenario Example: An example of how shifting the storyline may look on a practical basis.

Personal Reflection

In this chapter, your reflection will be ongoing as you read each thinking error. As you read through each type, when something stands out to you because you can relate, jot down notes about it in your journal.

Emotional Reasoning

Burns Definition: You assume your negative emotions reflect the way things really are.

Description: Emotional reasoning is the process of confusing an emotion with a static way of being or seeing something as fact. When you apply emotion as fact, you send the message to yourself that you *are* something rather than you are *experiencing* something momentarily. Feelings pass, change, or dissipate. "I am" is absorbed in the conscious and unconscious mind as though you *are* that description in your entirety and as a perpetual state of being. The mind then creates or adds to the story that nothing outside of this description exists or that you can't get out of this state of being.

Examples:

- I'm disgusting.
- I'm powerless.
- I'm not important.
- I'm trapped.

Buzzword(s): "I am" or "I am not."

Modification Techniques and Reframes:

When you say, "I am," and replace it with, "I feel," is this more accurate? If so, repeat the sentence but replace "I am" with "I feel." Then add details that more accurately describe the moment.

- "I am trapped" becomes "I feel trapped in this situation because my boss declines to meet with me."
- "I'm powerless" becomes "I feel powerless right now because I don't see any other viable options."
- "I am so stupid" becomes "I am really struggling with math. I don't understand it and have struggled with math since I was in the third grade. This subject makes me feel stupid."

Answer the question: Are you, in your entire existence at every moment, that description *or* are you experiencing an emotion right now that feels as though it has taken over your existence? If yes, then continue saying "I am." If not, specify what you are feeling.

- "I am inadequate" becomes "I feel inadequate for this job."
- "I am disgusting" becomes "I feel unattractive in this outfit."

When you identify the feeling(s), take a deep breath and acknowledge them. Breathing and acknowledging at the same time helps integrate and teach your body to validate you are experiencing a temporary feeling rather than a permanent fact.

Identify times when you do not feel the given emotion and acknowledge those times. If it benefits you to make a list of the examples, do so. Use the words "and" or "at the same time" to validate all pieces. This is extremely important to ensure you are acknowledging alternative evidence to broaden your story and more accurately state your truth.

- I feel inadequate at my job. At the same time, I feel really proud of my career growth and how I commit myself to learning to do my job well.
- I don't feel important right now because ____ canceled our plans. At the same time, I know I am very important to ____.

- I feel powerless right now. This situation feels so overwhelming. And I know I will find my strength because I have every other time in the past.

Scenario Example:

Manny has become good friends with a classmate named Susan. They have worked on several projects together and in that process have gotten to know each other well. Susan has said she enjoys hanging out with Manny. However, when Manny invites her to hang out for fun (rather than school projects), she always says she's busy. Manny finally gets upset one night and thinks to himself, I'm just not important to Susan. She says she likes hanging out with me, but she always says no when I ask her to hang out outside of school. *Manny then realizes he used "I am," so he examined if this was a cognitive distortion. He recognized that he stated something as fact "I am unimportant," but the more accurate statement is he* feels *unimportant to Susan in this moment. He does not know if he is unimportant to Susan. He challenged his thought by looking at evidence that she has always been honest with him and others, so she is likely being honest when she says she enjoys hanging out with him. In addition, he recognizes she is involved in several different extracurricular activities, so she is likely very busy outside of school. He, therefore, validates that he feels disappointed and worries he is not very important to Susan, and he recognizes that she may be telling the truth about being too busy to hang out.*

Labeling

Burns Definition: Labeling is an extreme form of all-or-nothing thinking [by] attaching a negative label to yourself.

Description: When you label yourself, you apply a single term to create an overarching theme or description of *who you are* rather than *what you did.* The labels are usually demeaning or do not recognize your positive qualities or successes. A label is appropriate when you are describing a defined role, such as being an "employee" versus the "owner" of a company. However, labeling is detrimental to self-worth when you use it to characterize your entire personality or existence with one limited description. Additionally, when you use a label, you train your mind to only see yourself through this one lens. You subsequently filter out times when you do not fit this label. This undermines your sense of self because you create the framework to only gather evidence fitting that description rather than recognizing and acknowledging the times when you don't fit that description. Labeling often accompanies emotional reasoning.

Examples:

Common labels will follow the format of a descriptive word such as stupid, lazy, failure, crazy, ridiculous, broken, burden, or worthless.

- "I know I am *ridiculous* for doing that."
- "I'm so *stupid* for dating those people."
- "I'm just not *good enough*."
- "I am a *burden* to others."
- "I'm *broken*."

Buzzword(s): Similar to emotional reasoning, "I am" or "I am not" is the primary indicator that you are using a label.

Modification Techniques and Reframes:

Examine what the label means. Define the label. Explore how you would describe it if you used that label on someone else. For example:

- What does it mean to be a failure? If you met "a failure," what evidence would you use to determine they were a failure?
- What does it look like to be good enough? What are the qualifications?
- What does it mean to be broken?

Challenge the "I am" just like you do with emotional reasoning. Do you *at all times* and *in every situation* fit that description (label) *or* did you just behave in a certain way at a certain time? This is the process of distinguishing behavior from a perpetual state of being. If you can answer "Yes, in every situation, I [blank]," then continue using that statement. However, if you can't, then adjust the thought to use sometimes, occasionally, often, or rarely. Adjust the label to describe more accurately what is going on. Does another description fit better, such as "falling short of my personal expectations" rather than "failing"? Or "My emotions are getting more activated than I would like. I would like to learn not to be triggered when this happens."

- "I am a burden" becomes "I feel like I have been burdening my friends and family recently by talking about all my problems."
- "I'm a failure" becomes "I am really upset that I made that mistake. I have been messing up often lately."

Ask yourself who gets to define the label. I like to ask the question, "Says who?" and explore responses to that question. This is often good to do through journaling. Most of the time, when people explore this question, they discover they don't actually agree with the original rationale.

- I am broken. Says who? Is there a universal definition of "broken"?
- I am a failure. According to whom and what standards?

If you have heard the label from someone else or received implied messages that others believe the label, ask yourself why they are important enough that they get to label you? Are they all knowing and/or do they have the final say. (Hint—no, they don't. Only you do.)

If more than one thing is at play or feels true to you, use "and" or "at the same time" to honor each piece.

- "I am lazy" becomes "I feel like I am lazy because I haven't finished my project yet. At the same time, I am earning straight As because of the effort I put into my work overall."

If the root of the label is actually based on fearing you are being a certain way or perceived a certain way, identify it as a fear rather than a fact.

- "I am crazy" becomes "I fear people will think I am crazy because of my PTSD symptoms."

Scenario Example:

Linda is a thirty-eight-year-old mother of two. She was raised by parents who subscribed to a very strict religion. She was explicitly taught that to be loved by God and accepted into heaven, she must behave in certain ways. When she made mistakes as a child, she was told by her mother, "God is so disappointed in you right now." From years of this message, Linda internalized that if she made certain mistakes, she was horrible and not worthy of God's love. Linda broke away from her church in her early twenties because she recognized she did not subscribe to the same beliefs. However, she still struggles with making sense of the internalized messages. Yesterday, Linda's boss yelled at her in front of her coworkers, so Linda was very upset when she got home. As the kids were getting ready for bed, her nine-year-old threw a tantrum and refused to get in bed. Linda's emotions welled up, and she yelled at her son, "Get in bed right now young man or you are going to be grounded for two weeks!" He got in bed and they said goodnight, but Linda was upset with herself the rest of the night for being so reactive. She felt a knot in the pit of her stomach when she went to her bedroom because she could hear her mom saying, "God is so disappointed in you, Linda," in her head. Linda then played out the typical narrative she had always struggled with: "I'm such a horrible mom. I am absolutely worthless." Then, she recognized these labels "horrible" and "worthless," because they were ones she had said many times. She then started journaling to reframe the situation. She recognized that she felt horrible for yelling at her son. She recognized that she wished she hadn't reacted like that. She then also recognized she had had a very emotional day, which was the underlying frustration that caused her to have less patience than normal. She also recognized it is normal to overreact, as all humans do it, and she trusts herself that she will take responsibility for it. She ultimately said to herself, "I messed up and didn't react how I would like. I am also a very good mother." She then made a list of reasons she is a fantastic mother.

All-or-Nothing Thinking/Overgeneralization

Burns Definition: You see things in black-or-white categories. You see a single negative event as a never-ending pattern of defeat.

Description: This is the pattern of classifying situations in absolutes and extremes. It exaggerates the situation and leads to filtering out acknowledgment of times when your behavior or experience did not fit the description. It contributes to extreme negative bias in how you see yourself.

Examples:

Here are some examples of all or nothing statements:

- I *always* mess up.
- I *never* get included.
- *No one* ever calls to ask how I am doing.
- He *always* lies to me.
- *Nothing ever* goes my way.
- *Everyone* is better at their job than I am.
- I am the *worst* football player.

Buzzword(s): All, none, everything, nothing, always, never, everyone, no one, everywhere, nowhere, worst, best.

Modification Techniques and Reframes:

Ask yourself: Is the use of absolutes an accurate statement in the situation? For example, is it true that you *always*, as in *every single time*, experience the described situation? If it is inaccurate, replace the polarized language with the appropriate description. Words that usually more accurately reflect a situation include sometimes, occasionally, rarely, once in a while, and often.

- "I'm always late" becomes "I am often late. I have a hard time getting ready quickly."
- "They never let me speak" becomes "They rarely listen to my side when they are mad at me."
- "They never invite me" becomes "Sometimes they don't invite me. Sometimes they do."
- "I am the worst player" becomes "I am not as good as some, and I am better than others."
- "I always fail" becomes "I struggle on most of my math tests. I have failed two of them and passed the rest."

If it is appropriate to add in "it feels like" or "seems like" to distinguish between feeling or perception and fact, modify the statement accordingly.

- "I am always messing up" becomes "It feels like I am often messing up lately."
- "I am always getting in trouble" becomes "It seems like I am always getting in trouble lately."

Breaking the one thought into multiple thoughts that name the opposing viewpoints is often the most accurate way to verbalize your perspective. Stating "and" or "at the same time" helps validate these opposing beliefs or thoughts. This is one of the most powerful changes you can make in your thinking patterns because so often we hold multiple beliefs at once.

- "I'm always left out of the group" becomes "I often feel left out of the group when we hang out together. At the same time, I feel included and important when I hang out with Becca."
- "I'm the worst dancer" becomes "I feel like I am the worst dancer on the squad. At the same time, I am one of twenty who made the squad, so I did better than sixty others."

- "I am never going to get over this breakup" becomes "I deeply miss hanging out with my ex. At the same time, I know the relationship was not healthy for me, and I am committed to taking care of myself."

Scenario Example:

Jon just received a text from a guy he went on a date with last weekend. The text reads, "Hey, Jon. It was good to meet you the other day. You seem like a really great person, and you are really fun. At the same time, I am not interested in another date. I just don't think we are a great match." Jon feels disappointed because he really liked this guy. He recognizes that in the past, he would be very upset and would be questioning his worth. Three years ago, he would be thinking, No one ever wants more with me. They always say I'm great, but I'm never good enough to date. *However, Jon has really worked through his narrative of "never being good enough to date" by acknowledging he has had a few relationships where he was very loved and recognizing there have been men he thought were great people, whom he didn't feel were a match for him. So, Jon responds from an honest, centered, and genuine place: "Thank you for your message. I appreciate you being open and honest. I am bummed. At the same time, I appreciate that you see my qualities, and I support you in knowing what you are looking for in a partner."*

Mind Reading

Burns Definition: You interpret things negatively when there are no facts to support your conclusion. Without checking it out, you arbitrarily conclude that someone is reacting negatively to you.

Description: Mind reading is pretty much what you think it is. It is creating a prediction of what someone else is thinking without having absolute evidence. It is a negative thinking pattern when you state it as fact but do not have solid proof of what the other person is thinking, feeling, or doing. More often than not, your prediction entails something negative.

Examples:

- I know she is mad at me because she hasn't returned my call from two days ago.
- The cashier thinks I am an idiot.
- The coach doesn't like me.
- My new boss thinks I am lazy.

Buzzword(s): For this type of negative thought pattern, I don't have any clear buzzword to point out. Recognizing this type of thought is done more by recognizing whether you are stating as fact what someone else is thinking or experiencing without having proof to back it up. "I know he/she/they think" would indicate potential mind reading.

Modification Techniques and Reframes:

Identify the objective and subjective information you have.

- Objective information is anything that is concrete, factual, and irrefutable.
  - They were laughing.
  - They used profanities when speaking to me.
  - They looked out the window as I talked.
- Subjective information is information shaped by perceptions, opinions, and interpretations. It lacks fact or proof.
  - She was smirking at me.
  - They weren't listening to me.
  - He had an attitude.

After identifying the subjective information, acknowledge/state any interpretation of that information or meaning making that you added without fact. Reframe your thought to include acknowledgment of your interpretation or meaning making.

- I am interpreting their comment to mean they are mad at me.
- I am worried they do not want to attend the event since they never responded.

If you are guessing someone is thinking negatively of you, make a list of alternative explanations for the behaviors you are interpreting or what may be going on with that person. Be sure to include possibilities that have nothing to do with you since this is often the case when we mind read.

- Maybe they are taking a nap and have their ringer off.
- Maybe they just had a heated discussion with someone else.
- Maybe they are more anxious and self-conscious than I am when they are out in public and, therefore, appear unfriendly.

Scenario Example:

Aaliyah just finished giving an oral presentation to her history class. She noticed three classmates had their heads down on their desks. She noticed people clapped at the end of her presentation but not "enthusiastically." When she ended her presentation and walked back to her desk, her teacher said, "Very good. Next." Aaliyah immediately wondered what others thought of her presentation. She theorized that her classmates were bored because of the students with their heads down. She guessed they weren't impressed with her presentation because they "barely" clapped. And she worried her teacher thought it was bad because all she said was "very good" and moved on to the next presentation. Aaliyah recognized she is "mind reading" and decided to challenge the evidence by coming up with alternative theories about what the class and teacher were thinking. She made a list of possible alternative explanations for the nonverbal cues and her teacher's words. Her lists included:

1. It is the last class of the day at 3:30 p.m. so people might be tired.
2. People might be similar to me and not be interested in history; therefore, it isn't about me but about the topic in general.

3. People are hot and tired because the air is not working today.
4. The teacher hasn't given any feedback to any student after their presentation so it might just be her style.
5. My topic was confusing to some people, which means it isn't about me, but the topic.
6. People have other things on their mind and aren't fully engaged.
7. I speak quietly so maybe some people couldn't hear me.

After this reflection, Aaliyah reframes her thoughts to, I worry that I didn't do well on the presentation and my classmates didn't like it. At the same time, there are likely other reasons in addition to my theories.

Fortune Telling

Burns Definition: You interpret things negatively when there are no facts to support your conclusion. You predict things will turn out badly.

Description: Fortune telling is the act of predicting something is going to happen without having evidence or certainty. Fortune telling can take place without evidence (i.e., my hair is going to turn green overnight while I sleep), or you may have had experiences previously that led you to believe the predicted situation can occur (i.e., you have been stood up before on blind dates). Fortune telling, when predicting negative outcomes, amps up your anxiety. You then operate from a place of fear and negativity rather than a place of safety and confidence.

Examples:

- I just know I am going to get fired for making that mistake yesterday.
- No one is going to invite me.
- They are going to be so mad about this that they are going to break up with me.

- If I wear this outfit, everyone is going to make fun of me.

Buzzword(s): The clearest buzzword is "going to." It might be prefaced with "I know that…."

Modification Techniques and Reframes:

Identify why you predict what is going to happen. What facts do you have to support your prediction?

Ask yourself, "Do I know without a shadow of a doubt that what I predict is going to happen?" If the answer is no, identify what other outcomes are possible.

Sometimes you have evidence that something is probable or likely. It is okay to validate that. In this situation, use the correct word, such as probable, likely, or possible.

- "Evan isn't gonna show up" becomes "Based on Evan's past, it is highly possible he will forget our appointment and not show up."
- "I just know I'm going to bomb this test" becomes "It's possible I could fail the test because the teacher makes the questions so hard."

If your prediction is based on worry or fear, name the emotion with the prediction. We all worry negative things will happen. It is best to acknowledge this rather than state something is going to happen.

- "I know they are not going to hire me" becomes "I worry I won't get the position."
- "This event is going to turn out awful" becomes "I am scared things are going to go wrong."

Take time to think through other possibilities. Make a mental list or write down a list of potential outcomes.

Scenario Example:

Damian is finally ready to talk to his dad about his feelings regarding a conflict they had a couple of months ago. Before talking to his dad, Damian tells his brother about his plan. His brother immediately responds, "Why are you even going to bother? You know Dad isn't going to take any responsibility, and he is just going to get angry." Because Damian has been processing this in therapy, Damian replies, "Yes, I recognize it is probable Dad is going to be mad. And yes, it is possible he is going to deflect responsibility. At the same time, I have learned new ways of expressing myself. I would rather attempt to talk to Dad to resolve this, knowing his patterns, than assume that things won't get better and just give up." Damian also admits to his brother, "I do feel some fear and apprehension. And I believe it will be better for me to try to address it."

Should Statements

Burns Definition: You tell yourself things *should* be the way you hoped or expected them to be.

Description: "Should" is a word "used to indicate obligation, duty, or correctness." Should statements come in the form of should, need to, or must. These "shoulds" are often based on unrealistic or unfair expectations. There are actually very few "shoulds" that make sense. One "should" I can get behind is, "I should pay my electricity bill." Yes, that is probably a really good idea because if it doesn't get paid, the electricity will be turned off. Most other times, should statements point to unhelpful expectations. Then when you fall short of those expectations, you internalize not being good enough or doing things right.

Examples:

- I should just stop caring and getting upset.
- I just have to get up and do it.
- I should have never taken this job.
- I need to stop being so anxious.
- I shouldn't have let myself develop feelings for that person.
- I must figure out how to work seventy hours a week like my coworker.

Buzzword(s): Should, should have, need to, have to, must.

Modification Techniques and Reframes:

Explore where your expectation comes from. You can do this by asking yourself who determines this "should" is a reasonable or appropriate expectation of you. For example, you realize you are saying to yourself, "I should be married by now." So ask yourself, "Says who?" Then ask, "Why do they get to set this standard?" Explore whether you agree with this expectation and/or the rationale of the expectation. Decide if this expectation matches your values, life circumstances, capabilities, and personality. Also think about whether you are fairly evaluating yourself in comparison to others or whether you hold higher standards for yourself that you would never hold for someone else. If the expectation doesn't match you or your life, modify your thought to match your reality.

- "I should be married by now" becomes "Aunt Elma grew up in a generation where people got married in their teens even if they were not ready or healthy for each other."
- "I should own a house by now" becomes "I have received messages from society that I should own a house by now, but I have prioritized spending my money on traveling the world so that I can understand what others' experience."
- "I shouldn't have gotten divorced" becomes "The church says divorce is wrong, but I didn't enter into a marriage agreeing to abuse. I needed to get out for my survival."

As you identify your expectations through your should statements, recognize your underlying desire or goal. Then modify your thought to reflect your wishes. This creates a mental framework of possibilities rather than restrictions. Substitute your should statement with:

- It could be beneficial if I....
- I would like to....

- My goal is to….
- I want to….
- I am working toward….
- I prefer if I….

Many times, when we place expectations on ourselves, we are doing it because we believe it is the right thing for us to do. However, we may not be fully on board with the expectation because it is not in complete alignment with what we want. Therefore, if you have competing desires, acknowledge them with "and."

- "I should just make exercise a priority" becomes "I would like to get into a daily routine of exercising, and I am struggling to fit it into my schedule because I don't want to spend time away from my kids if I don't have to."
- "I need to just sit down and get my project done" becomes "I want to do well in school, and I am exhausted from having a full-time job at the same time so I want to rest."

When you are struggling with "shoulds" from past choices, reflect on who you were and where you realistically were at the time you made your past decisions. Think about what you knew or didn't know at the time. Validate how you made the choice based on the knowledge, skills, and resources you had at the time.

Scenario Example

Melissa has dated Brad for four years. She met Brad during her senior year at the University of Colorado. When they graduated, Brad got a job offer in North Carolina. They decided to stay together and move. Just last week, Brad told Melissa he no longer wanted to be in the relationship because he realized he doesn't want kids, and he knows she wants a family. She knew he was on the fence early in the relationship, but they were so young when they got together that she did not put much weight on the issue. Melissa called her sister to tell her about the situation, obviously feeling upset. She told her sister, "I've wasted all these years in the wrong relationship. I should never have gotten together with him. I should have known better than to fall in love with someone who wasn't sure they wanted kids." After letting out her emotions as her sister listened, Melissa took a deep breath. She recognized she was buying into a lot of "shoulds," so she used the tools she had learned. She modified her thoughts to "I am extremely sad that our relationship is ending. I love Brad. And part of me worries I wasted crucial time I needed to find my right partner. At the same time, he and I did not know ourselves as well back then and focused on other positives in our relationship in the decision to pursue it. We made the best decision for ourselves at the time."

Personal Reflection

1. Which type(s) of thinking patterns do you struggle with the most?
2. Write down a negative thinking error and walk through the steps and examples to practice modifying the thought.
3. Identify and work through as many negative thinking errors as you want.
4. Create a journaling ritual to identify and work through these errors until you can recognize your negative thinking errors quickly. (Note: You can download some really helpful apps to do this regularly.)

Avoiding Toxic Positivity

In the United States, we have a horrible problem with sugar-coating things and insisting that putting a positive spin on things is the best way to live. This is known as *toxic positivity*. I like verywellmind.com's description of toxic positivity: "Toxic positivity is the belief that no matter how dire or difficult a situation is, people should maintain a positive mindset. It's a 'good vibes only' approach to life. And while there are benefits to being an optimist and engaging in positive thinking, toxic positivity instead rejects difficult emotions in favor of a cheerful, often falsely positive, facade."

Examples of toxic positivity:

- "At least they are in heaven now."
- "Just look at the bright side: At least you didn't get fired."
- "Everything happens for a reason."
- "God won't give you anything you can't handle."

I believe it is valuable to identify positives. However, these types of phrases inhibit a culture from talking openly about life's difficulties. They can also imply someone is bad for feeling negative emotions. This creates more internal isolation and feelings of inadequacy or brokenness.

When talking about reframing your thoughts, I am not talking about "looking at the positive" and, in effect, denying or invalidating the negative. I also do not advocate stuffing down emotions. Besides, you are your own BS detector, so you cannot fool yourself by telling yourself lies, including positive ones. If you can identify something positive that you actually believe, allow both the negative and the positive to be present. This means remembering *and.* For example, with losing Ashton, my thoughts are that I believe he is in heaven, for which I am grateful. *And* I would prefer that he was still with me here on earth.

Writing Your Own Story

Imagine you open your browser and see the headline, "Two vicious dogs sent to the pound because their owner couldn't handle them." What sticks out to you as valuable details? What impression do you get about the dogs based on the adjective "vicious" and that the owner "couldn't handle them"? They sound like unruly pups, right?

You decide to read the article and discover the dogs are pit bull mixes (if you know pit bulls, they are some of the sweetest dogs), and they are at the shelter because the owner got into a car accident. The owner is severely injured and will need months of physical rehabilitation and feels the dogs deserve a home where they can be taken care of properly.

The words used in the headline are drastically different from the content of the story.

Words matter. Words particularly matter when it comes to writing your own story. One of the greatest contributors to damaged self-worth is when your negative thoughts, through your words, become sentences. And the sentences become paragraphs. And the paragraphs become chapters. Until one day, you believe an entire negative story about your value.

This proves that if you change the words and sentences that make up your beliefs about yourself, you can shift your entire story. While this process can be potentially slow and difficult, depending on how rehearsed your internal dialogue is, you hold great power to modify your narrative.

If you were to write your autobiography today, what would the title be if you only listened to your negative self-talk (like my old story, *Amanda, the Worthless Piece of Shit*)? Which thinking errors contribute to your storyline? And now, after learning and practicing how to modify the thoughts to integrate facts and evidence, what would the story include? If your story focused on separating feeling from fact, what would it say? If you allowed for many things to be true at once, using "and," how would this change the content of the chapters? If you were to intentionally look for evidence to support new perspectives, what would you see in your life?

Growth Activity

What is the story you want to write about your life? Create your title and outline of your book. Use the following prompts for ideas:

1. What title would honor your worth?
2. What chapters honoring the challenges you have encountered are important to include?
3. What chapters acknowledge you being in the process of healing?
4. What chapters honor your resilience, strengths, and triumphs?

Changing the Way You Talk to Yourself

Learning to change the way you talk to yourself by modifying your thoughts is a game-changer, but it takes a lot of practice to recondition your thoughts. This won't happen overnight. At the same time, I guarantee as you shift the way you talk to yourself, you will start shifting the lens through which you see and experience yourself. You will be able to regulate your emotions better and feel more at peace. While you did not create the storylines based on thinking errors, you are now in charge of what you do to define your true story and the story that comes next. Your anxiety will decrease. You will feel more in control and capable of navigating tough situations.

In the next chapter, you will explore strategies for seeing yourself through a more positive lens by identifying your strengths. This process will further support your ability to change your thoughts. It will create a reciprocal relationship you can use to identify all aspects of the truth about what you contribute to this world, not just seeing or focusing on the negative. By recognizing your strengths, you will continue to build confidence in who you are and your worth.

CHAPTER 4
Owning Your Strengths

"Greatness is not this wonderful, esoteric, elusive,
god-like feature that only the special among us will ever taste;
it's something that truly exists in all of us."
— Will Smith

Anyone who knows me well knows I am a crier. Almost anything can make me cry because my body is just built to produce tears when I feel intense emotion. I have very little control over my tear ducts and the chemical buildup that produces my tears. If someone tells me not to cry, I am incapable of stopping.

This bodily response has historically been unwelcome or unappreciated by others. I have received many direct and implied messages about my crying. As a child and young adult, I was expressly told (by multiple people) I was "too sensitive." Sometimes I got in trouble for crying. Some people would roll their eyes. I was told countless times, "There is no need to cry right now." None of these comments helped me cry less or become "less sensitive." In fact, because I felt hurt by the criticism over something I could not control, I would normally end up crying more. Whenever I was scolded for crying and strictly told to "stop," I would try my best to hold in my tears. But that would create severe stomach aches and anxiety. Once I was allowed to be alone, I would cry for hours upon hours.

From this criticism and inability to control my bodily response, I internalized that I was broken. I started believing I was inherently problematic for feeling strong emotions. This chipped away at my sense of worth. All I wanted for years was not to be "so sensitive." I would beg God just to help me "not care so much" about things.

Another major personality trait others criticized, thus adding to the evidence that I was built wrong, was being an "overthinker." I have been told hundreds of times, "You think too much." When I explained this was just something that happens, I was told, "Well, just stop doing it." I eventually started replying, "If you know where the 'off' switch is, let me know, and I will gladly use it." I know I am not alone in this experience because many clients have told me they have heard the same criticism. Can you relate? Do you wish there were some magic switch you could turn off?

By internalizing that crying and overthinking meant my body is built wrong, because other people told me I "should" function differently, I innocently added this evidence into the belief that "I was not good enough."

Thank goodness I eventually discovered my truth. I learned to see the beauty in these traits and value these pieces of me. When I cry, it represents my ability to feel deeply. My tears are a symbol of me having the gift of empathy. Because I am comfortable with crying, I am able to make space for others who are in pain. Friends and loved ones know they can come to me with anything, and I won't tell them to stop crying or get over it.

Regarding "overthinking," I know my ability to assess and think through things thoroughly has been a great asset to me, particularly in my professional life, and it has also helped others. For example, I remember one time I was in a meeting with about five colleagues, including other coordinators and directors. They were going round and round discussing ideas. All the while, I was silent and listening. After about thirty minutes, the director turned to me and said, "Okay, Amanda, give it to us. What should we do? I know you have been putting all this together as you listen and are thinking ten steps ahead." That was a very powerful and validating afternoon. Rather than being seen as defective for "overthinking," I was recognized for having a strength in listening, paying attention to detail, and foreseeing future outcomes to assist in coming up with a solid strategic plan for our company.

Another aspect to my personality I came to identify as a strength was realizing how many times I heard "stop analyzing me" from others. This confused me for a couple of years. I knew it was because the person knew I was a therapist. Yet I realized these people thought I was analyzing them to judge them (to determine what they were doing or whether who they were was good or bad). After reflection, I realized the purpose of my "analysis" was quite the opposite. It was to compassionately understand them, to meet them where they were. It was quite the opposite of judging them.

As my recognition of my gifts grew, I was able to see where I was useful and how I could use my gifts for good. It helped me navigate situations in which I used to compare myself to others and feel less than them. I saw how each of us in the situation contributed in unique and valuable ways. I was able to seek and commit to situations in which I could expand on my strengths. It helped me come to know myself so that even if someone misinterpreted my actions, I knew my truth and intentions. And last, instead of hiding, I discovered opportunities where I could shine.

Looking Through a Strength-Based Lens

For several years in my career, I worked with youth who were on probation for committing crimes. I will never forget one client who was on probation for stealing a car. I previously had clients who had secretly taken the keys from someone in their house and then taken the car for a drive. This situation was different. This client stole a random car by breaking in and hotwiring it. He then drove the car to a junkyard of sorts and sold the parts.

Hold up! How does someone hotwire a car? How does a sixteen-year-old know how to do this?

Maybe it's not "hard" to start a car without keys. I honestly have no idea. What I do know is that most people don't know how to operate a car without keys. Yet this client did.

My initial reaction wasn't, "Wow, what a horrible person. They don't respect others' property!" (Don't worry; we addressed respect for others' property.) Instead, I was fascinated by the skills it took to scope out a car, unlock it, start it without keys, drive it without being pulled over, and then have the business skills to sell it.

This client had been labeled a "bad" kid. He held this identity because he had been told he was bad for years by family, teachers, and other adults. Therefore, instead of harping on him for making poor choices, I helped him begin to recognize the skills he employed to accomplish what he did. I assisted him in recognizing his knowledge, such as how car parts work together. We identified the interpersonal skills that helped him sell the car. Once we made an inventory of all his strengths, we looked into professions in which he could apply these strengths, such as car mechanics, engineering, sales, and business planning. It was the first time this kid ever recognized he had qualities and skills that could be used for good. All I did was look at the same situation through a different lens to identify what he did well.

As you read the rest of this chapter, I invite you to look at yourself through a similar lens. A strength-based lens recognizes things you do well (skills), values and virtues you use to guide your actions, and personality traits.

Personal Reflection

To jumpstart the process, in your journal, write a list of strengths you recognize right now. You can include ones you confidently believe you have and ones you sort of believe. As you proceed through this chapter, add to the list when you recognize something else.

Misunderstandings About Strengths

Some common misunderstandings exist about strength-discovery and taking ownership of your qualities. Read through these so you can be equipped to handle your thought processes as you get further into discovering your strengths.

Misunderstanding One: "Naming my strengths is arrogant or suggests I am better than other people."

This misconception comes from a very good place. It means you value avoiding being or acting superior to others. It means you value being humble. Recognizing your own strengths *does not* mean you believe you are better than others. The two are not synonymous. You can recognize a strength in yourself and still be humble. Improving your self-esteem by recognizing all that is special about you is not going to make you forget how to be humble. The fact that you are even worried about it indicates it is not likely to happen. In addition, the better you get at recognizing your strengths, the more compassion you may have for those who are struggling. This is the opposite of arrogant. Further, the more you learn to celebrate your strengths, the more you will celebrate the strengths in others.

Misunderstanding Two: "I have/had no choice."

Let me illustrate what I mean through an example. I give someone a compliment on focusing so much energy on providing a safe and stable upbringing for their child. This person responds, "I didn't have a choice. That's what parents do." This is not accurate. Not all people choose to provide for their children. This example is applicable if you rationalize that you had no choice in doing something that is seen as a strength. You choose to do it. Something within you opts to use the skill. It may be that the consequence(s) of not doing it may be too great, such as the parent who chooses to show up because the child would suffer otherwise. However, it doesn't discredit, diminish, or negate the fact that you choose to act.

Misunderstanding Three: "Everyone/anyone can do this/be this way."

I'm not trying to be flippant, but if anyone can have a strength, why don't they? Sure, humans have great capacity to build strengths, but not every person can do what you do. Some people do not have the same capabilities as you. Some people may not have the same access to resources to build that strength. And some people may not choose to build or use the skill or quality. None of this is meant to pass judgment on someone else or create a sense of inferiority/superiority. Either they do not have the capability, they don't have access, or they choose not to. The task or skill might seem easy to you or extremely common. However, this does not diminish the fact that you have the strength. The more you learn to recognize and appreciate your capabilities, the greater your ability to teach and support others in building similar strengths.

Misunderstanding Four: "This quality is not a big deal or special."

Thinking about misunderstanding number three and that not all people have, employ, develop, or expand the skill, if you actually think about it, then for those who possess the quality, it is special. But regardless of the uniqueness of your skills or their quality, it matters. If a child came up to you and proudly showed you how they started riding a bike without training wheels, would you say, "So what? Other people can do that too"? No, you would praise them for it. You would be excited for *them* and what it means for *their* life. As you grow into adulthood, your strengths don't diminish in value. All your strengths are worthy of being embraced and honored. What good is life if we can't celebrate the things that make us who we are?

Misunderstanding Five: "But it's the right thing to do, so it doesn't deserve recognition."

How many of society's problems are connected to people not doing what is right? People commit crimes knowing what they're doing isn't right. People lie knowing it's not the best way to handle things. So why diminish your recognition of doing what's "right"? Feel proud that you *choose* to do what is moral.

Misunderstanding Six: "My bad qualities discount my good qualities."

We all have desirable and less-than-desirable qualities. They coexist. *But* our imperfections don't discount our positives. When you play with a child who has the gift of laughter and play, and then they make a mistake in the game, do you think they are completely bad? Does their mistake take away from their qualities? What about someone you love? Since everyone is imperfect, you know they have some less than ideal qualities. But do you discount their worth by saying because of those bad qualities, the good ones don't count? No, you appreciate and love the whole being. So, you can also love your whole being.

Personal Reflection

Which of the six misunderstandings above do you relate to and/or struggle with? Where do you think the misunderstandings came from? What can you do to help remind yourself of the truth about your strengths?

Skill Recognition

We will start by recognizing strengths equated with skills. First, we will look at the milestones you have achieved and the skills it took to achieve them. Review the list of milestone examples below to recognize the skills associated with each. Remember, any level of capability deserves recognition. If you did the activity, you possess the skill. If you have not yet achieved the milestone but are in the process, look at the skills you are currently using to work toward the achievement. Break down the actions that led to achieving or completing the task or goal. Be specific about the steps you took.

Milestone	**Skills**
Completing an educational program *(i.e., high school, college, technical school)*	• Completing assignments • Organizational skills to get tasks done • Researching information • Retaining information in some fashion • Studying for tests • Juggling school responsibilities with your personal life and responsibilities • Stress management • Self-discipline
Receiving a license for a job *(i.e., cosmetology, electrician, real estate)*	• Retaining the information • Practicing the tools • Displaying competency • Memorization • Consistency in learning or doing
Getting hired for a job	• Filling out an application appropriately • Writing skills for resume, cover letter, or written questions • Critical thinking in interview • Assertiveness in interview • Willing to take risks with interviewing
Maintaining employment	• Showing up consistently and on time • Completing required tasks • Meeting expectations of boss/company • Abiding by company policies • Demonstrating reliability of meeting expectations • Showing consistency in behavior to maintain employment • Interpersonal skills with coworkers
Receiving a promotion	• Demonstrating leadership skills • Demonstrating reliability • Demonstrating consistency • Demonstrating quality of work

The next area of recognition is looking at the skills you use currently. Each of us do so many things daily that take skill, but we are not encouraged or supported to slow down and really think about the skills involved in getting those things done. Begin by reviewing the last list to identify any skills that are applicable to your life now. Then read the list below to add to your list.

Additional Daily Living Activities	**Skills Likely Required**
Daily living skills	• Paying bills • Organizing finances/budget • Grocery shopping and meal planning • Maintaining household chores • Managing time to show up to scheduled activities and obligations • Taking care of your personal health (physical and mental)
Maintaining relationships *(i.e., friendship, roommate, romantic partner)*	• Bonding • Showing care and interest • Communicating • Negotiating differences • Empathizing • Following through with commitments • Allowing yourself to be vulnerable
Caretaking of others *(i.e., children, family members)*	• Organizing schedules • Providing for their wants and needs • Multitasking • Anticipating needs • Getting them resources (i.e., to doctor appointments) • Managing stressful situations

Value-Driven Behavior

Another lens through which you can identify your personal strengths is to assess what you value and the subsequent behaviors you engage in to live in accordance with that value.

If you value…	You might have the ability to…
Caring for others	• Empathize • Listen intently • Anticipate others' wants and needs • Give of your time and/or resources • Show warmth and kindness • Refrain from judgment
Resolving conflict with others	• Take ownership of your behavior • Display courage to confront someone even though it could be uncomfortable • Display openness to understand the other person • Listen to feedback • Provide constructive feedback • Regulate self to handle the discomfort • Tell the truth
Fun	• Use creativity to come up with things to do • Act spontaneously • Find joy • Feel grateful for opportunities • Take risks
Social Justice	• Stand up for others • Assert yourself • Evaluate what is humane and ethical • Examine problems on a larger scale • Think critically about how policies affect people and systems

The more consistent you are in your behaviors, the more confident you feel in your abilities. Additionally, others will associate you with these skill sets and qualities. They will get to experience your authentic, confident self and be more drawn to you.

Surviving Adversity

I have heard "You are so strong" hundreds of times. I've even heard, "I could never survive what you have." I know these statements are meant as compliments, but I don't love hearing them. I don't like my "badges of honor" because I have experienced great pain and loss to gain them. The way I have learned to be strong is a consequence of things happening that I wouldn't wish for anyone to go through.

At the same time, here I am overcoming adversity.

And I am damn proud of it!

Since you picked up this book, it isn't far-fetched for me to assume you have been through at least one significant hardship. Perhaps you experienced abuse, bullying, racial oppression, or poverty during childhood. Whatever the life challenge, you deserve recognition for making it this far. I want to invite you to honor your resilience and perseverance. I hope you can feel a sense of pride for choosing to make it this far. Strengths worth recognizing likely include your abilities to:

- Regulate your nervous system through stressful times
- Seek and use help from other resources
- Function independently
- Lead and/or care for others
- Compartmentalize to stay focused on survival tasks
- Stay committed to moving forward

I predict you may also minimize the intensity of what you have been through. I get that. I have done that as well. In my experience, the most common reason that people minimize or discredit their strength and resilience is to avoid claiming superiority to others. However, honoring and recognizing what you have overcome does not indicate you believe you are better than others. It merely honors the challenges you have tackled and the effort you have put in to survive. Of all the things worth commending in this world, I believe choosing to get up and keep putting one foot in front of the other is the greatest strength of all time.

Growth Activity

1. What are you proud of? This could be any level of pride, even just "I'm glad I was able to do that."
2. Imagine you meet someone who wants to accomplish exactly what you did, but they have no idea how to do it. Write them step-by-step instructions.
3. Read each of those steps and absorb "I did that." "I am capable." "I was able to."

Bonus Growth Activity

Recognizing strengths in others helps us recognize and appreciate our own strengths. So, in the next week, identify three people in different parts of your life whose strengths you will consciously notice. Write about their strengths in your journal at the end of the week. Give yourself bonus points if you include someone who irks you or gets under your skin because they, too, have strengths and deserve recognition.

Navigating Future Situations

While it can be beneficial to have the ability to think ahead, we all experience way too much stress by worrying about the future. We create anxiety in ourselves by predicting negative experiences. I have spent a lifetime learning to worry less, and I have found that at the root of all worries is the *fear* of *not being capable* of handling something. So, when you are feeling anxious about something in the future, it's not your fear of the outcome; it's your fear of your inability to cope with the outcome.

If the source of the anxiety is fearing your capability to handle the situation, then one tool to help you work through this is to identify your strengths and evidence of your abilities. Let's look at these situations to get a clearer picture of how turning around your awareness of your capabilities can play out:

Anita has been invited to a party but only knows the host. She says "yes" to the invite, but as the event gets closer, she starts to feel anxious. She thinks to herself, I'm nervous that I won't know many people. *Upon breaking down what makes her nervous about not knowing many people, she realizes that she fears:*

1. *No one will talk to her so she will be standing in a corner all alone.*
2. *Others will judge something about her and think negatively of her.*
3. *She will clam up and not be able to make conversation with others.*

Anita realizes each of these fears boil down to her fear of rejection or not belonging.

If we look closer at this scenario, it's not that Anita fears rejection in and of itself. She likely has experienced rejection without feeling bothered about it in other situations, such as when someone doesn't smile back when waiting in line at Starbucks. The root of discomfort is the fear she won't be able to handle the perceived rejection well, that she will take their lack of engagement personally and then will battle thoughts of not being good enough. So, what could be helpful for Anita is to remember times when conversations went well with new people. Perhaps even remember when she made new friends as a result of meeting them. She could also reflect on times she engaged in conversation with others from a confident and calm place. She could also explore the times she was not affected by rejection because she did not buy into the idea that their rejection said something negative about her.

Raul (nonbinary) is exploring the possibility of moving to a new city. They write down a list of pros and cons and ultimately determine that moving to a new city could be a great thing for them. Then, later that night, they imagine quitting their job and putting in their notice to end the apartment lease. All of a sudden, they feel tremendous anxiety. Raul decides to journal to identify the source of the anxiety. They realize that not knowing anyone in the new city and not having a social life is the cause of the stress. On even closer examination, Raul pinpoints the fear that loneliness might lead to a depressive episode.

When Raul moves, it is accurate that they will have increased alone time in a new city for a while because of not being as connected socially. But when Raul acknowledges the worry of not being able to handle increased alone time, Raul brainstorms ways to spend their time in the new city. They also plan how to take extra self-care measures to combat potential depression while he works toward building social connections. Raul remembers previous times of successfully managing depression, so they feel more confident of being able to do so when they move.

Jayce is upset with her brother, Joel, because of something he said the other day that felt insensitive. Jayce talks to a friend about the situation who suggests talking directly with Joel about it. Jayce instantly feels anxiety upon hearing this suggestion and says, "No, I can't do that." The friend asks, "Why not?" Jayce explains that often when Joel is called out on his actions, he gets defensive and argues. The friend inquires further, "Why is his defensiveness and arguing a problem for you?"

Jayce reflects on her friend's questions and realizes she fears she will become emotional and cry in response to Joel's argumentative nature. Jayce also fears shutting down if the discussion becomes too activating.

Jayce decides to brainstorm ways to proactively handle the situation by making a list of her personal strengths when it comes to having difficult conversations with other people. She knows she is able to do this at work all the time as a customer service representative. Jayce also decides she can tell Joel ahead of time that when she gets too activated, she shuts down, so that they can plan on possibly taking a break if it goes in that direction.

It is perfectly normal and understandable to feel nervous about future situations. We all experience this. Once you recognize exactly what you fear you "won't be able to handle," you can then plan accordingly. You can identify which strengths and skills will help you during the anticipated situation. Then, you can look back at similar situations to remind yourself you have done it before so you can do it again.

Another tool that can be helpful when you feel worry, fear, or apprehension around a future situation is to give yourself permission to "worry" about it as time gets closer to the potential event. This sounds like, "I will figure it out when I get to that point." Giving yourself permission to plan around the situation later can minimize the time you spend ruminating on "what if?" scenarios and can buy you time to remember your capabilities. You can also tell yourself, "I have navigated this before. I will be able to do so again when the time comes."

Showing Up Fully

One of the greatest gifts of recognizing and owning your strengths is it directly influences how you show up in your life. When you feel good about what you do or proud of your traits and recognize what you do well, you will engage more fully in opportunities. This engagement ends up creating so much more meaning and fulfillment.

Think of an activity in which you feel you perform poorly. Or think of a situation where you feel timid, insecure, or self-conscious. Bring one of those situations to mind and notice what it feels like in your body. Notice your lack of enthusiasm for doing it. Notice how your posture turns inward or your back tenses up. Notice the self-talk and criticism associated with the thought of being in that scenario.

In contrast, think of situations where you were fully engaged and confident. Think of times when you were not focused on or concerned about your shortcomings because you were either enjoying yourself or feeling good about your skills. What is different in these situations? What are your thoughts like? How does your body feel? What strengths are you aware of?

When you recognize, embrace, and feel pride for your strengths and qualities, you show up more fully in life. You will access more courage to try things. You will enter situations feeling confident, centered, and energized rather than anxious and desiring to hide or play small. From there, you will connect deeper with others. You will make bolder moves to go after your goals and achieve your dreams.

Growth Activity

Did you know that in many ways our brain responds the same to imagination as it does to reality? This is why visualization can be so powerful. Think of a situation that makes you nervous and where you would like to be more confident. Perhaps it could be a job interview, a speech, or a social gathering. From the list of strengths you gathered earlier in this chapter, close your eyes and visualize using those strengths in the future situation. If you want, write out the visualization first, as if you are writing out a movie script. Then put on some relaxing music, get comfortable, close your eyes, and visualize the process of owning your strengths and showing up more fully and confidently.

Bonus Growth Activity

Google "strengths inventory assessment," and you will find a few options to complete an online assessment to identify additional strengths. I personally value the book *Now, Discover Your Strengths* by Gallup, Buckingham, and Clifton. This book includes an access code to complete the Clifton StrengthsFinder 2.0 Assessment. This assessment really helped me see myself through a different lens. Another popular strengths assessment can be done through the VIA Institute on Character at www.viacharacter.org.

Love Your Qualities

You are special. There is only one you for a reason. The more you see your beauty, the more you will show up differently in the world. You will make decisions from a place of confidence and trust in yourself. You will attempt goals you used to be too scared to pursue. You will be able to quiet the negative voices in your mind telling you that you aren't good enough for that promotion or you aren't attractive enough for that person to choose you because you will know your value. You will learn to dance as if no one is watching, and if they are watching, they will see your beauty because you see it and shine.

In the next chapter, you will learn techniques for setting the standards for how others should treat you. This will enable you to invite people into your circle who have earned the right to be there because they see your beauty and respect your well-being.

CHAPTER 5
Standing Up for Yourself

"You will never gain anyone's approval by begging for it. When you stand confident in your own worth, respect follows."

— Mandy Hale

With all the uncertainties in the world, one thing is guaranteed: You have yourself, and you are with yourself forever. In your lifetime, you can be your worst enemy or you can learn to be your best advocate. Advocating for yourself includes how you stand up for yourself. You set the tone for how others treat you.

When you do not fully believe you are worthy of love, it shows in how others treat you. This is because you allow patterns of behavior from others that do not align with treating you respectfully. Perhaps this is because you do not feel important enough to be treated well. Or you may think poor treatment from others is normal because no one has shown you better.

Fully embodying your worth cannot be accomplished without learning to set boundaries around how others treat you. As you stand up for yourself, you open doors to rewarding and safe relationships that reinforce your worthiness.

Frozen in Silence

One lunch hour in sixth grade, I walked up to my regular group of friends. The eight of them were standing in a circle with their backs to me. As I approached, everyone turned to look at me and became very quiet. The "queen bee" of the group broke the silence by saying, "You're kicked out of the group. You can't hang out with us anymore." When I asked why, she said, "Because we don't like you." Everyone else remained silent. Most of them just looked down at the ground to avoid eye contact. I stood there stunned as tears welled up in my eyes.

I had been friends with these girls for a few years. I went to all their birthday parties and sleepovers. They came to my house often. I talked with some of them on the phone daily. Two of them considered me a best friend. And then, without warning or explanation, I was told I was no longer "allowed" to hang out with any of them. I was so confused.

My spirit broke into pieces. In a matter of minutes, my belief that I was not good enough solidified further. My twelve-year-old self learned that not only did my dad not want me around as much, but something was so wrong with me that multiple "friends" also no longer wanted me in their lives.

When this happened, all I did was turn and walk away. I didn't ask more questions to understand. I didn't protest. I didn't tell any teachers or counselors. I continued to treat those girls nicely and somehow put a smile on my face. Some of the friendships reignited the following year, but I never told them how incredibly painful the experience was. Instead, I was so happy to be "accepted" again that I didn't address it. I healed in some respects with these friendships, but the "not good enough" wound from this outright rejection impacted me for years.

I was already a passive and accommodating child in many ways, but this ostracism really set the tone for my future of not standing up for myself in relationships. I deeply feared if I stood up for myself and called others out for their uncaring behavior, I would be "thrown out" again.

In response to this experience, I developed another survival strategy: be the most supportive, loving, and helpful friend a person could have. I made it my mission to "love and give to others no matter what." I genuinely gave to others, so I wasn't faking it. But unconsciously, I was driven to go above and beyond in relationships because it created a sense of safety. I discovered if I provided something helpful, they were less likely to leave me or reject me.

"Love and give to others no matter what" came with a price, though. Over time, my loving others "unconditionally" included:

- Prioritizing others' wants and needs over mine, even if it meant giving them the shirt off my back and me ending up naked.
- Forgiving others without asking them to take responsibility for their actions.
- Permitting excuses from others for poor behavior, rationalizing that good intentions and good hearts outweigh their hurtful choices.
- Hiding or withdrawing my voice.
- Blaming myself or inappropriately owning other people's actions.

By not standing up for myself and prioritizing others, when things became too much for me, I would ask for (or even try to demand) too much from others. I set expectations of others that were too high, so they inevitably disappointed me. I lacked understanding of their boundaries and even disregarded them. I took it personally when they set boundaries, thinking, *Well, I always do this for you; why can't you do it for me?* Eventually, this ended up costing me a few friendships, which was exactly what I was trying to avoid.

As I began to transform my life after my breakdown in college, I realized I needed to learn how to treat myself as though I was worthy of love and respect. I needed to set the standards for how others could treat me. Major shifts began once I became my best advocate.

Self-Preservation and Self-Honoring

As you go through this chapter and read about techniques for standing up for yourself, I predict you will at some point think, *I can't do that; that would be selfish*, or something along those lines. It is extremely common for people to have the misunderstanding that standing up for themselves means being selfish. "Selfish" is defined as "lacking consideration of others; concerned chiefly with one's own profit or pleasure." In other words, to act "selfishly" is to not care about others and only to be concerned with your own gain.

Yes, this chapter focuses on teaching you ways to take care of *your* wants, needs, and desires. However, it does *not* include ways to disregard others, exert power over others, or take advantage of others. Therefore, these techniques are not about teaching you to act selfishly. Standing up for yourself is not about putting others down, but instead elevating yourself to the same level as them.

I classify behaviors that align with standing up for yourself as either self-preserving or self-honoring. You likely have heard "Don't jump in the pool to save someone if you can't swim." The advice is to throw in a life preserver so you stay safe *and* the other person gets out safely. This illustrates the concept of "self-preservation." Self-preservation is necessary. In this analogy, it makes no sense to jump in to save someone if you can't swim, because more than likely, you would both drown. In many instances, standing up for yourself is essential to self-preservation. To not stand up for yourself could cost you your life. Think about someone who is intoxicated getting in the driver's seat of a car, and they ask you to get in the passenger side. Saying "no" is not selfish but self-preserving.

Expanding beyond self-preservation is what I call self-honoring. These are the actions we take that honor the truth of our essence and individuality. Self-honoring entails acting in alignment with our values, our preferences, and our opinions. Self-honoring actions may not be pleasing to others. They may not be understood by others. However, they are actions that serve us best in the long run. Both self-preservation and self-honoring behaviors include consideration of others, and ideally, negotiations to meet both parties' needs and wants.

Personal Rights

Does anyone deserve to be physically assaulted? Does anyone deserve to be demeaned with insulting language and name calling? Does anyone deserve to have their voice completely silenced? Does anyone deserve to be treated as though they are inferior to someone else?

If your answer is "no," but you endure behaviors such as these, why is that? Why do we humans sometimes tolerate poor treatment?

The primary reason I can identify is that something in your life muddied the waters of you either knowing your personal rights or believing that there are people who can and choose to fully respect your personal rights. Perhaps you were raised in a culture that supports "putting others first." Or maybe you experienced childhood abuse that taught you when you make a "mistake," you deserve to be physically punished. Or perhaps you are part of a marginalized group that has less access to rights and resources compared to the majority. Whatever the culprit behind you not knowing your personal rights or not believing you deserve the same treatment as others, I want you to know that *you*, as a human, have the right to:

- Be physically safe and free from physical violence
- Protect yourself mentally and physically for your survival and well-being
- Act independently and autonomously
- Take care of your own needs
- Attain your own goals and dreams
- Have your own opinions, thoughts, and emotions
- Express yourself and use your voice
- Choose whom you surround yourself with

You do not have to earn your personal rights. You being alive and human is reason enough. Babies don't enter this world needing to earn these rights.

These rights are inherent to existence. So, why should you lose these rights as you age?

Personal Reflection

Being curious and compassionate about your life, journal on these questions:

1. What were you taught (directly and indirectly) in childhood about your personal rights?
2. What current messages do you get, interpret, or experience that say you do not deserve to have your personal rights respected?
3. What gets in the way of you standing up for your personal rights?
4. If you believe you are less deserving of your rights being honored, what thought modifications could you explore to arrive at believing you are just as deserving as any other person?

Whether you believe your personal rights matter or you know they matter but you don't know how to stand up for them, learning to put yourself first regarding these rights is vital to standing in your worth.

Understanding Boundaries

"Boundaries" was not a common term when I was younger. It wasn't a concept we openly talked about or recognized. Today it is part of many people's daily language and often highlighted as something to understand because people generally know that boundaries are "good" and that "we all have the right to set boundaries." At the same time, a lot of confusion still exists about boundaries. Most people I interact with struggle to fully understand what boundaries are or how to create and implement them. That is because we live in a world that sends incredibly mixed messages about boundaries, and few households accurately and actively teach children how to have and maintain boundaries.

So, what are boundaries? In the simplest terms, boundaries are limits. In reference to human interaction, they are limits we set between one another to honor each other's safety and autonomy. They are what we use to stand up for our personal rights and respect others' rights.

One of the most influential books I have read is *Boundaries* by Dr. Henry Cloud and Dr. John Townsend. They reference the idea of owning a property, such as a house with land and a fence to distinguish the area as your property. They describe that boundaries help delineate what belongs to whom. They say, "Boundaries help us keep the good in and the bad out."[1] It is your responsibility to learn what your limits are and to stand up for them so you can keep the good in and the bad out.

Boundaries are established through various forms, which may include:

- The physical body, such as if you decide to engage in personal touch
- Time, such as if you want to see someone soon or wait to engage with them later
- Physical space in the manner of literal distance between one person and another (one foot or 2,000 miles)
- Words, such as saying "yes" or "no"
- Metaphorical space, such as deciding to get close to someone emotionally

Boundary Patterns

Within the framework of boundaries, people engage in three types of boundary patterns. The first pattern is *rigid* boundaries. This is when you have very firm boundaries and little flexibility. When I think of the property analogy, I imagine a brick wall as the border with electric fencing on top. On this rigid property, the door of the house is made of steel and has

1 Cloud, Henry and John Townsend. *Boundaries: When to Say Yes, How to Say No to Take Control of Your Life*. Grand Rapids, MI: Zondervan, 1992. p. 33.

twenty different locks. Basically, almost no one gets in, and if they do, they have to jump through a bunch of hoops to get to you.

Examples of rigid boundaries might look like:

- Only wanting things done a certain way while not being open to feedback or alternative ideas.
- Only dating people who match specific criteria and not giving anyone a chance if they don't meet this criteria.
- Not sharing any personal information or vulnerabilities with others so as to not build emotional intimacy.

Rigid boundary patterns are not to be confused with firm limits and expectations about personal rights, such as requiring consent to engage in physical intimacy or not allowing violent behavior.

Enforcing rigid boundaries is rooted in an innocent attempt to keep yourself safe. The strategy is to keep pretty much everything "out," leaving minimal chance of getting hurt. It is essentially over-protection. As with any strategy, it serves a purpose at some point. However, over time, having too rigid of boundaries can take a toll on your relationships and self-worth because it can create a sense of isolation, judgmental feelings toward others, or distrust that others have the capabilities of adding something positive to your life. Therefore, it is beneficial to assess if you have rigid boundaries that prevent you from letting the good in.

The second pattern is *soft* (or open) boundaries. This pattern is characterized by a lack of boundaries and/or lack of clarity about your boundaries. On this property, there is no fence and the front door is open for anyone to walk in. You don't have consistent rules about who gets in or out.

Examples of soft boundaries include:

- Saying "yes" when asked to help with something even though it interferes with your plans.

- Always allowing others to choose where to go or which activities to do even if you dislike it.
- Not expressing when something hurts your feelings or offends you as you continue to engage with that person.

It is probably no surprise that I will again state: This boundary pattern is also innocently rooted in an attempt to keep yourself safe. The strategy, much like how I described my own history, is to keep others "in" so they don't leave or reject you. This comes at the expense of also allowing the bad in. It often stems from trying to avoid upsetting others, particularly if you anticipate you will suffer consequences if you set a boundary. For example, you may not want to express your opinion to your parent if you anticipate that they will respond with the silent treatment for days.

The trouble with a pattern of soft boundaries is that over time it sets the tone for others to prioritize their needs or wants over yours. People may learn to take advantage of you or take you for granted. They may also receive implied permission to mistreat you. Think of the phrase, "Silence is compliance." By being silent and not setting boundaries about who and what gets in, you become complicit in not being treated as equally important. This could lead to feeling resentful, unimportant, or invisible. These feelings then ultimately continue to wound your sense of worth.

The boundaries to strive for are *flexible* boundaries. These boundaries aim to mutually respect your and others' safety and well-being. Creating flexible boundaries entails seeking to understand yourself and understand the other person. You then seek to meet in the middle. You learn to be clear within yourself about your wants, needs, and responsibilities. You then communicate clearly to others. You remain open to hearing their wants, needs, and desires.

Consider this scenario that illustrates flexible boundaries:

Margo needs a ride to the airport tomorrow. She asks her friend Annette to take her at 8:30 a.m. Annette looks at her schedule and sees she has a meeting at 9 a.m. She tells Margo, "Yes, as long as I can drop you off at 8 a.m. so I can get to my office in time for my 9 a.m. meeting." Margo and Annette both express their needs and find a solution that works for both of them.

Another example of flexible boundaries might look like:

Eric and Iza are roommates. They begin to talk about household chores, and quickly, the discussion becomes contentious. When Eric gets activated, he wants to find a resolution as quickly as possible. When Iza becomes activated, her thoughts begin to race and she can no longer think straight. They both know this about each other because they have been longtime friends, so as soon as Eric recognizes that Iza is becoming flooded, he offers that they take a twenty-minute break to re-center. Iza agrees that this could be beneficial for her. They agree to reconvene in twenty minutes and finish their conversation so that Iza is able to have her break and Eric can feel better that they have resolved the problem sooner rather than later.

When you are flexible with your boundaries, you recognize each person has a right to their opinions and needs. You recognize their stance is not a reflection on you but how they try to take care of themselves because you recognize you, too, are just trying to honor yourself. You feel a mutual respect by acknowledging you are both autonomous humans just trying to work through a joint situation.

Personal Reflection

Your boundary patterns stem from what you were taught (directly and indirectly). They are likely also connected to a survival strategy of some sort. For example, if you got in trouble for voicing opinions, you may have created the pattern of being accommodating and prioritizing others. Or if you were consistently abused or disregarded, perhaps you created rigid boundaries to keep others away.

1. How did your boundary patterns come to be?
2. How do they protect you and help you survive?

3. What compassion and validation can you give yourself and/or your younger self regarding how these patterns came to be?
4. How do you desire to modify your boundary patterns in the next few months and why? (Remember to honor the *and*, allowing for wanting to be safe *and* desiring to move in a different direction.)

Growth Activity

This drawing activity will allow you to explore your own boundary patterns through visualization. Visualization through art helps the mind process information differently than just reading words. This is not an art contest, so there is no good/bad or right/wrong. (When I do these things, I use a mix of drawing and words to depict what I am exploring.)

1. Take a twelve- by eighteen-inch piece of paper (or similar size to have enough space) and colored writing/drawing tools.
2. Draw your property type, such as a house, a pool, or a building.
3. Draw the type of entry to this property that symbolizes the people you let into your space.
4. Draw the border to your property. What is it made of? How tall is it? How thick is it?
5. Draw or write words that represent the good you let in (or don't) and the bad you keep out (or don't).
6. After you have reflected on your current personal property and feel ready, then draw or create a vision board of what you want to let in and keep out as you learn to strengthen your boundaries.

The Responsibility Backpack

Imagine waking up each day, and as soon as you open your eyes, you put on an invisible backpack. You wear it everywhere you go. In this backpack you carry only what you have control over. This includes things like the choices you make, the words you use, and the opinions you hold. Now imagine others carrying a personal backpack as well that holds what they control and have influence over.

One of the best ways to fully understand how to set boundaries is to be clear about what you are responsible for. Boundaries break down when personal responsibility is in the wrong backpack, either because you inaccurately expect someone else to take responsibility for something that is yours to own or by taking ownership of something that actually belongs to someone else.

Inside Your Backpack

- Your words. They are a primary source of communication. It is up to you to communicate your thoughts and feelings. People cannot read your mind.
- Your nonverbal communication. This includes body language, tone of voice, and volume. Nonverbal communication makes up the majority of our communication. It is up to you to ensure you are communicating what you mean.
- Your responses, either verbal or behavioral. It is your responsibility to manage your responses and accept outcomes that are natural reactions to your responses.
- Your choices. No one makes you do anything. You weigh the pros and cons of choices and act accordingly.
- Your feelings and how you manage them. No one can take care of your emotions. You are responsible for identifying them, processing them, nurturing them, and regulating them. It is nice when others can support you through them, but ultimately, they are your responsibility.
- Your questions. If you are unclear about something, if you are interpreting something, and if you are lacking information, it is up to you to clarify by asking questions.

- Your explicit expression of the existence of your boundaries, needs, desires, and opinions. You cannot expect others to automatically know what they are, even if they seem obvious to you.
- Your handling of things today and moving forward. You cannot change the past.
- Your self-care. This includes physical and mental health, whom you let in, and the goals you pursue.
- Your internal thought process. You get to examine your thoughts and how you gather information to form your thoughts and opinions.
- Your boundary enforcement. Others cannot enforce them for you. You must be the one to stand up for yourself.
- Your respect for others' rights and boundaries. If someone sets a boundary, you have the option to respect the boundary. When you respect others' boundaries, they are likely to respect yours.
- Your willingness to ask for help. Some people may come without you asking, but most will not. If you want support or help, it is up to you to ask.
- Your alignment with who *you* are. This is your life, your journey. You get to live it how you desire and see fit.

Inside Their Backpack

- Their words. It is not up to you to read other people's minds. If they do not communicate, it is not your job to guess. If they do communicate but don't communicate exactly what they mean, it is not up to you to know the difference. It is their responsibility to clarify.
- Their nonverbal communication. It is not up to you to guess what their nonverbals mean. It is their responsibility to communicate to you the meaning of their nonverbals if there is confusion.

- Their responses, either verbal or behavioral. It is their responsibility to manage their responses and accept the outcomes that naturally follow their responses.
- Their choices. You don't make anyone do anything. They weigh the pros and cons of choices and act accordingly. Don't take the bait if they tell you otherwise.
- Their feelings and how you manage their feelings. You cannot take care of someone's emotions. You can be kind and cautious about how you behave in consideration of someone's feelings. But they are not yours to own, process, or manage.
- Their questions. If they are unclear about something, if they are interpreting something, and if they are lacking information, it is up to them to clarify and ask questions. You cannot read their mind to know what they are thinking, assuming, or confused by.
- The communication of their boundaries, needs, desires, and opinions. It is not your responsibility to know all these things if they have not told you.
- Their actions today and moving forward. They cannot change the past. It is up to them to take responsibility. And they cannot rewind.
- Their self-care. You cannot force them to take care of themselves. When we love someone, we want the best for them. At the same time, they are responsible for honoring their own well-being.
- Their boundary enforcement. They are responsible for standing up for themselves. You can support them if they are open to it. But they still are responsible for enforcing boundaries and accepting the outcomes if they don't.
- Their choices even if you may not agree. They get to choose what works for them. That doesn't mean you have to continue the re-

lationship if what they choose disrespects you or no longer aligns with your life. But they still get to choose how to operate.

If you have been conditioned to take responsibility for things that don't belong to you, know that you are not alone. There are so many unhealthy cultural and intergenerational norms that confuse boundary ownership or support displaced boundaries. Therefore, it make take time to learn what only belongs in your backpack and what you rightfully can separate as belonging in someone else's backpack.

Let's walk through a few scenarios that illustrate responsibility ownership. When you read each scenario, think about who might be responsible for what. These scenarios are not for assigning blame or judging any character. Instead, they are meant to heighten awareness of who is responsible and, therefore, who can make different choices. After each scenario, you will be asked reflection questions. If it is helpful to you, refer to the above lists to answer the questions.

Juan is the adult son of Maria. Juan calls his mother to talk about Thanksgiving plans. He asks his mom if it would be okay for the family to have Thanksgiving dinner at his house since it is the first Thanksgiving he, his wife, and his newborn will be living in their new house. She says, "Well, it has always been at our house. But yeah, I guess that's fine." Juan hears her sigh when his mother says this, so he asks, "Are you sure?" She says, "Yes, we will go to your house." A few days later, two weeks before the holiday, Juan texts his mother, "We are just finalizing details for Thanksgiving. Are you still cool with it being at our house?" She responds, "It's fine." Thanksgiving Day comes, and Juan's mom and dad arrive at his house. While they are cooking, Juan says some people will have to eat in the living room since the dining table only has room for four people. Juan's mother sighs and says, "Well, if we had had Thanksgiving at our house, this wouldn't be a problem. I really wanted it at our house, but that wasn't an option." Juan leaves the room feeling as though he has disappointed his mother and thinks to himself, I should have known she wasn't okay with this.

Scenario Reflection

1. Which actions belong in Juan's backpack?
2. Which actions belong in Maria's backpack?
3. How is Juan taking more responsibility than belongs to him?
4. How is Maria not taking appropriate ownership of her actions?
5. What could either of them have done differently to ensure each person takes appropriate responsibility for what they can control?

Brayden is the ten-year-old son of Mike. On Monday, Brayden tells Mike he has a school project due on Friday. Brayden tells his dad the project is to create a presentation board on five places Brayden wants to visit. Mike says, "That sounds cool, bud!" Thursday night rolls around and Brayden says, "Hey Dad, I have that project due tomorrow. Can you help me with it? I have picked out the pictures I want to use so I will need to use the printer. I also don't have a posterboard to put them on." Mike hears this and yells, "Brayden! It's Thursday night, and you are just now telling me? The printer is out of ink. Now I have to go buy ink and get poster board." Brayden begins to cry, and says, "I'm sorry, Dad." Mike responds, "You are so irresponsible. This is inexcusable. I expect you to do these things ahead of time." Brayden continues crying, "I'm sorry, Dad; I didn't mean to."

Scenario Reflection

1. What were Brayden's responsibilities in this scenario?
2. What were Mike's responsibilities?
3. How could Mike have modeled navigating ownership of responsibility with Brayden in a clear and compassionate manner?

Sam is a nonbinary twenty-one-year-old. Sam texts their friend, Adam, to ask if he can meet up over the weekend to play Dungeons and Dragons. The two text back and forth discussing plans. Saturday comes, and at around 11 a.m., Sam texts Adam to inquire about when they will hang out. Adam doesn't respond for hours. Around 2 p.m., Sam's sister calls to ask if Sam wants to go to a movie. Sam texts Adam again asking, "Hey, are we gonna hang out?" Two hours pass and still no word from Adam, so Sam agrees to go to the movie with his sister. They leave thirty minutes later to make the 5 p.m. show. When Sam comes out of the theater and checks their phone, Sam sees three texts from Adam. "Hey. What time are we hanging out?" "Hello?" "Guess you ditched me. Thanks a lot." Sam immediately texts Adam, "I was at the movie with my sister. Just got out. I tried to get a hold of you. Can you still hang out?" Adam doesn't respond. Sam texts again the next day, "Hey what's up?" Adam reads the message but doesn't respond for several hours. He finally texts back, "You ruined my night. I don't think we can be friends anymore. I don't want to be friends with people who ditch me for better plans."

Scenario Reflection

1. How did Sam take responsibility in this scenario?
2. How did Adam attempt to displace responsibility?
3. What could have been done differently by either Sam or Adam?

Empathy and the Responsibility Backpack

As you become aware of your personal backpack, it is important to notice and be aware of how your choices and behavior interplay with other people's experiences. What you say or do affects others. The effect and interplay differ with each individual and are influenced by factors such as personality, the type of relationship, and life experiences.

Recognizing your separate backpacks and knowing others have their own does not absolve you from doing your best to be aware of how your actions affect others.

While it is important to gain clarity and skill in only owning what is yours and setting boundaries so others own what is theirs, this does not mean to take on an attitude of, "Well, it's their problem if they get upset." It is still important to be aware of how your actions interact with someone else. It does not mean to become unempathetic, because lacking empathy in a relationship or exchange isn't ultimately helpful. Lacking understanding and not caring about someone else's patterned responses with an attitude of "They need to deal with that themselves" can break down trust and caring. We still have a responsibility to treat others with respect.

Think of someone you know who might be a little more sensitive when it comes to feedback. Perhaps as a child they received copious criticism and little positive feedback. Maybe when they hear criticism, they believe it means you disapprove of them and no longer want to be a part of their life. I encourage you to think wisely in such cases about how you give feedback. The way you say something inevitably influences your friend. It is not on you to necessarily manage their response, but if you are aware of their soft spots, you may choose to approach the situation a little more gently than you would with someone else. If they interpret your words incorrectly, perhaps you might be willing to invest in a little more clear communication and explain where you are coming from.

The "You Made Me Feel" Error

How many times have you said or heard, "You made me feel [blank]"? It is a common belief that others make us feel a certain way. I believed this for many years because it seemed like something outside of me made me feel emotions. The reality is what others do influences us. But others don't *make* us feel a certain way. Our feelings stem from our own thoughts and the meaning we make of what is said.

Imagine you are dating someone you respect and appreciate, but you don't see them as a romantic partner. You anticipate it would hurt their feelings if you broke up with them, so you stay silent and keep the relationship going. You fear if you break up with them, you will *make them feel* unloved or inadequate. The truth is they may feel sad or hurt. However, if they interpret the breakup as meaning they are unloved or inadequate, then that is on them. It is up to them to work through the experience and not add their own meaning to what you communicate.

If you get into a situation in which you believe someone else *made* you feel a certain way, recognize that they did not force emotions on you. They acted, and your interpretation and experience of the event led to a certain emotion. This doesn't mean you are being unreasonable for having certain thoughts and subsequent emotions in response. For example, if your best friend excludes you from a social event, it is understandable to feel hurt. But if you then feel unimportant, your friend did not make you feel this way. You arrived at this feeling because you interpreted the exclusion as meaning you are unimportant to the friend. It's your responsibility to examine and understand the thoughts and stories causing your emotions.

You don't want to get caught in the trap of believing others cause your emotions because it creates (or adds to) a sense of powerlessness. As intense as emotions may feel, you are not powerless.

Boundary-Setting Techniques

The most common question I get once someone recognizes they need to set a boundary is, "But how?" The reality is I could write a completely separate book on boundary-setting techniques. And yes, setting boundaries can be difficult. I learned how to establish boundaries over many years of practice. Sometimes I still need reflection time or help with clarifying my boundaries and how to stand up for them. Use the guidance described next to work toward stronger boundary setting.

Identify the Underlying Purpose of Your Boundary

Begin by identifying the purpose of the boundary you want to set. Essentially, define the *why* behind the boundary. Is it to stand up for your personal safety? Is it to express your opinion? Is it to establish an expectation of behavior? When you clarify the purpose of the boundary to yourself, it will be easier for you to communicate the boundary to someone else.

- I am setting this boundary to clarify that I will not engage in an argument that includes name calling.
- I am setting this boundary to establish what I will be in charge of because it's within my abilities.
- I am setting this boundary to communicate that I cannot fulfill this role of mediator between my parents.

Delegate Responsibility

Identify what you are responsible for and is in your control (what belongs in your responsibility backpack) and what the other person is responsible for (what belongs in their backpack). The clearer you are with this, the easier it will be to find the words to verbalize your boundaries.

- I am responsible for how I deliver my opinion when I call them to discuss the situation.
- I am responsible for being honest when they ask me about my experience.
- They are responsible for asking me questions if they do not understand what I am saying.
- They are responsible for telling me they are overwhelmed and need a break.

Identify Your Thoughts and Emotions

Identify your specific thoughts and emotions so you can clearly articulate them when the time comes. The better you understand your thoughts and emotions, the better you will be able to match your verbal and nonverbal communication with what you want the other person to hear and understand.

- I wondered if your deep sigh meant you were upset. So then, I felt frustrated at you not communicating with me because I don't like to make assumptions. I'd prefer you tell me directly how you are feeling.
- I feel unappreciated because I don't receive praise when I complete an assignment. I'd appreciate more positive feedback.

Use "I" Statements

When you are ready to communicate your boundaries, speak only for yourself using "I" statements. "I" statements demonstrate you are taking responsibility only for yourself. You are owning your feelings. You are owning your thoughts. You are owning your preferences. You are fully standing in your power and honoring yourself. You are refraining from blaming. Powerful "I" statements sound like:

- "I do best in a work environment that allows time for me to ask questions."
- "I do not tolerate people calling me names."
- "I ask that we take a break if one of us gets so triggered we start raising our voice because when someone speaks to me with a raised voice, I shut down and can't think straight."

Be Objective and Concrete

If you need to point out someone's behavior to clarify something or set a boundary, use objective, concrete, and observable descriptions. Avoid judgmental, subjective, or critical language because it just puts people on the defensive and will likely divert the conversation to them defending against your judgment rather than creating space for a constructive solution.

- "I'm tired of you saying rude things about people." Instead, say, "You used the word 'bitch' the other day when describing a coworker. I'm asking you not to use that word in front of me."

- "You acted ridiculous the other day." Instead, say, "I felt really uncomfortable when you raised your voice at those people yesterday."

Keep Things Simple

When in doubt, keep your statements short and simple. You do not owe people long explanations. So many people have been conditioned to think they must justify their boundaries. The truth is your boundary is all that needs to be stated for the other person to understand your request or expectations. Examples of being concise and to the point include:

- I need to take a break.
- I only want to invite family to the party.
- I cannot meet at that time.

Ask for What You Want

Know that you have the right to your preferences and the right to ask for them to be honored. You are not wrong for asking. It's up to others to decide if they can and would like to honor that boundary. It is up to them to ask questions if they are confused about your request. It is also on them if they get offended by you asking.

- "Telling me I can turn it in whenever is not helpful for me. What would be helpful is setting a deadline. Is that possible?"
- "Instead of going on Monday when I typically have my painting class, can we go on Tuesday?"

Personal Reflection

Think of a recent situation that has activated (upset) you in some way. Practice "I feel" statements. If it would be helpful to you, search the internet for "a feelings list" so you can identify the most accurate emotions. Emotions that are often felt but overlooked or unrecognized include abandoned, rejected, ashamed, or betrayed.

Growth Activity

Take an outing this week to a park or somewhere you can practice identifying concrete, objective, and observable behavior. Write all the descriptive words that come to mind as you observe. Examples include "a person shrugged their shoulders" or "a person turned their body away." The more you practice naming objective behavior, the easier it will be to communicate when you are in boundary-setting conversations.

Understanding Pushback from Others

As you begin to stand up for yourself in new ways, you will likely get some pushback from others. They might view your actions as selfish. They might get defensive. This is completely normal. It happens because of humans' innate drive to maintain homeostasis (keep the system operating the same). You changing the dynamics all of a sudden may feel unsafe to the other person, so it may take time for them to confirm you are still a safe person with new boundaries.

For many years, I interpreted others setting boundaries as either a form of disapproval or as withdrawing love. But I will never forget the powerful aha! moment when I began to learn the true lesson of boundary setting. It happened during my senior year of college when a friend said, "I love you, and I cannot engage in this dynamic between us anymore." She carried on to name my behaviors that she would not tolerate. I finally understood the distinction that her love for me was separate from her dislike of my behaviors. I was able to respect her decision to set boundaries about my behavior in our relationship. This was when I began to understand not loving a behavior of mine is not synonymous with not loving me. This friend distanced herself as a way to set boundaries. When I felt sad or guilty, I repeated her words in my head, "I love you, *and*," to retrain my wiring to understand love in the heart and dislike of a behavior can co-exist.

You, too, can reassure others as you shift your boundaries with them. You can clarify that your care for them is separate from your experience or opinions about their behavior. You can explain that boundary setting is not you judging them; it is merely you honoring your preferences. You can still feel and express empathy for their situation or where they are while telling them they are not allowed to be harmful in your life. You can clarify with something like, "I like you. I just don't like this behavior." Or you might say, "I'm not invalidating your emotions. I am setting boundaries about how you handled your emotions with me."

I would not have predicted learning to respect other people's boundaries and discovering my own would bring tremendous peace into my life. When your actions consistently align with who you really are, what you really feel, and what you really value, you experience less anxiety. You begin to feel secure because you know you are being consistent and true to all parts of you. This will then have a ripple effect on your relationship with others because they will also experience you as consistent, honest, and authentic.

The additional benefit of self-honoring is the more you honor yourself, the more you will model and encourage others to honor themselves. You will be supporting them in standing in their power. And you will both learn that self-honoring does not have to be confrontational; instead, it can create more harmony because you both understand that to honor yourself does not mean you don't honor someone else.

You Set the Stage

You have the right and responsibility to live in alignment with your needs, preferences, and desires to ensure you function optimally. Doing so is the only way you can create a better life for yourself. You are the change-agent in your life and responsible for being your best advocate and fully standing in your worth as a human.

How you stand up for yourself then directly impacts the types of relationships you will have. When you stand in your power, you interact with others from a grounded and healthy place that enables you to have healthier and more satisfying relationships. In the next chapter, you will learn powerful tools for building these healthier relationships.

CHAPTER 6
Building Healthy Relationships

"You have to meet people where they are,
and sometimes you have to leave them there."
— Iyanla Vanzant

Humans are designed to be in community. When it comes to self-worth, relationships are critical to our well-being. Relationships impact how we feel about ourselves and the enjoyment (or lack thereof) we feel in our lives through connection. When we engage with people who embrace us and treat us well, they reflect our value back to us. Conversely, if we participate in unhealthy or disruptive relationships, we suffer. Poor relationships are probably the biggest source of injury to self-worth, particularly when others tell us or imply something is wrong with who we are.

Because relationships so strongly influence our sense of identity, the people we choose to be in relationships with and how we participate in those relationships matters. Learning to pick who we want to include in our life and how we interact with others enables us to discover our value and supports us in standing in our worth.

The People We Invite into Our Lives

When it comes to relationships, I cannot express enough gratitude for the people in my life. I have so many beautiful relationships with family and friends. Many of my friendships are decades-long. I have deep friendships with people all across the United States, and I continue to make connections. It surprises me sometimes that there were moments in my life when I felt completely alone and unloved, but this could not be further from the truth now. I know how blessed and loved I am today.

At the same time, I had a rough journey developing romantic relationships. I used to have an amazing knack for (unconsciously) pursuing emotionally unavailable men. I spent nearly twenty years attracted to men who either said they weren't ready to date or who verbalized they were open to a relationship, but their actions did not support the claim. I also had a long history of tolerating and excusing selfish and unloving behavior from men. I didn't allow abusive or unfaithful behavior. But I did put up with thoughtless actions, half-assed engagement in the relationship, and being the placeholder until they met the person they wanted to be with long-term.

One of the most harmful patterns I permitted was investing in relationships with guys who said all the right things about valuing me and behaved like we were in a relationship. But they didn't want an actual "relationship" with me. The first guy in this pattern once wrote me a card that said, "I can't begin to tell you how happy I am that we have become such close friends this year. I feel so lucky to have you.... Thanks for all the smiles this year and all the smiles to come." His words accompanied hand-holding, cuddling, and hanging out on a daily basis. Then out of nowhere, he asked some other girl (whom he had never mentioned) to be his girlfriend. The last man in this pattern said I was a "diamond in the rough" followed by "but I don't want a relationship" after months of talking about what our future together might look like. The number of times I heard, "You are amazing and will make some man so lucky one day," followed by, "but that man is not me," is more than I can count on both hands. While that can be a beautiful compliment, with my deeper layer of not believing I was "good enough," all I internalized was "You're good, but not good enough for me because there is someone else better for me out there." I stayed in those relationships experiencing moments of love but overall inadequacy.

I know most of these men really cared for me. I don't doubt that. And not finding me to be their match for a lifelong partnership was not a problem. The problem was I gave of myself in unhealthy ways. I committed to them, but they didn't commit to me. I put up with all sorts of behaviors that reinforced my low self-worth. Honestly, I allowed myself to tolerate some pretty shitty behavior because they told me how much I meant to them. For example, some would make plans to hang out with me and then cancel at the last minute because they got a date with someone they wanted to pursue romantically. I convinced myself this was okay with thoughts like, *I want them to be happy* and *It doesn't mean they don't care about me*. Those were partly true, but deep down, it reinforced the belief that something about me made me unworthy of their romantic love.

I was caught up in this pattern time and time again, starting in college and up to age thirty-six for a few reasons. One was my subconscious attempt to re-story my relationship with my father, Lee. Having the false belief that I was not good enough for my dad, I was replaying the relationship to try to achieve a different ending and be chosen. My subconscious believed if I could finally have someone choose me, it would prove I was good enough in the end. This belief is actually a common psychological phenomenon known as *repetition compulsion*.[1]

I also engaged in this pattern because I really believed for a long time I must be inherently unworthy of being chosen because something was wrong with me. I felt as if others could somehow see a major flaw I wasn't aware of, but they wouldn't tell me what it was. Part of me even theorized that for some reason God didn't believe I was supposed to have a partner. I feared maybe I was meant to be alone forever. As a result, I stayed in relationships because I believed they were the best I deserved. Why should I

---

1 https://www.psychologytoday.com/us/blog/anxiety-zen/201603/why-do-we-repeat-the-past-in-our-relationships. Accessed March 10, 2023.

bother asking for more or better if I didn't believe I deserved it or couldn't find it?

But then, right around my thirty-sixth birthday, I experienced a transformative moment when I made the conscious decision to change this pattern. I was talking to my mom on the phone, processing my pattern of getting attached to another man who claimed he cared about me (the one who said I was a diamond in the rough) but didn't want to commit to a relationship. I recognized that my belief I was undeserving of a relationship was a fear, not a fact. So I took ownership that when I acted from this fear, I allowed partnerships with people who did not treat me as fully worthy. With the realization that I was the one tolerating less than what I deserved, I declared thereafter I would only date men who wanted to commit to a full partnership. I decided I would only consider men who were clear in their intentions of finding a life partner. I acknowledged that I still felt skeptical of my worth, but I would only allow relationships that aligned with me being worthy. I made the conscious commitment to myself to play the role of someone who fully believed in herself and believed she, too, was deserving of a healthy, loving partnership. I decided to stand up for my worth.

A few months later, in 2015, the journey with my soulmate began.

This cannot be a coincidence. I believe with every ounce of my being this declaration to embody my worth through action (even though parts of me were behind in believing my worth) opened the door to finding the perfect man for me. This man, Kevin, knows and reflects my worth. He always treats me as lovingly as anyone deserves to be treated. And our relationship is the healthiest, most vulnerable, and most connected relationship I have ever had. In turn, the relationship with him has helped me become an even better person and helped heal many pieces of my heart. Our marriage is better than anything I dreamed of. My heart feels more full than I ever thought possible.

You're the Driver

I invite you to imagine you have decided to go on a road trip. For this trip, you plan to drive across the country. This means the trip will take several days. It will include various elements that will affect your enjoyment throughout the trip, such as how you want to spend your time while driving (i.e., listening to music, audio books, or talking with someone).

The key question: Who do you take with you?

Do you take someone who will talk your ear off the entire time? Do you choose your guest based on musical preferences? Do you take someone who will boss you around and dictate when you can stop for a bathroom break? Do you take multiple people with varying personalities and strengths? Do you invite someone who can share in the responsibility of driving?

You are in the driver's seat of your life journey. Because you're the driver, you get to decide who comes along for the experience. You can decide who gets access to you and which parts of you they get access to. Keep this in mind as you explore your relationships and take charge of your journey.

Authentic Self

If someone were to inventory all the books in the world, I hypothesize that the most common theme in them would revolve around being in relationships with others. As relational beings, this makes sense. It further makes sense because it is extremely difficult to live completely isolated from other people.

With all the tools that already exist to aid in navigating relationships, I think the most important piece of guidance is *to be 100 percent yourself.*

So many of us are trained to not be our authentic selves because we live amid cultural norms that promote putting on masks, catering to what others want, or fearing the judgment of others' opinions. Think of photography, for example. Many are trained early to "smile for the camera."

This reinforces a message that you should put on a front for others to see. Another common message is "It's not okay to cry." People are explicitly told "Don't cry" or "Oh, there is no need to cry right now." Watch reality TV for one week and you will see this occur countless times. These messages get internalized as: It is bad to show your true self.

But it is impossible to have a fully healthy relationship if you are *not* being yourself. Your true self is not meant to be hidden or shoved into a box. Therefore, you can only endure putting on a front, hiding parts of you, and swallowing your voice for so long before your soul demands you honor and reveal your true self.

Think about driving the car on your road trip. Imagine you have a strong sensitivity to scented items. With some scents, your eyes become irritated and dry. You decide, however, not to tell the passenger beforehand because you fear offending them or pushing them away.

Then let's say they get in the car wearing a scented hair product. Even though you don't say anything, your sensitivity is not going to disappear. What's going to happen? Your eyes are going to get itchy and impair your ability to drive. Ultimately, you will most likely have to tell them you are having an allergic reaction because your body did not cooperate with hiding it.

Now imagine you tell the potential guest about your sensitivity before you select them to go with you. This can feel scary if you predict they will judge you or react negatively. At the same time, at least they know what you need and then have the option not to come along or to modify their products for the trip. If they don't want to come or don't want to make adjustments, at least you know before it becomes a problem.

Being authentic does not require you to show all of your cards if someone has not earned the right to know you at that level. However, with the information you do choose to reveal, you can be true to yourself.

The more honest you are with yourself about who you are, the more able you are to be upfront with others about what you bring to the table. From this authentic and honest place, you will find people with whom you align faster and easier. I have personally discovered I much prefer to show who I really am from the get-go so I can weed out anyone who isn't going to support me. Life feels so much easier when I do this because no one's time is wasted on hoping or expecting me to be someone I am not.

Vulnerability

Many of the things I am inviting you to do require vulnerability, or in other words, require you to take risks. Vulnerability can feel uncomfortable or even scary if you think about it in terms of potentially being rejected or judged by others. It is not fun to grapple with someone deeming you to be good or bad, worthy or unworthy, and it can be extra difficult when you struggle with your own judgment.

At the same time, I know, without a shadow of a doubt, that when you choose to take those risks and reveal your true self, you open the door to experiencing one of the most precious gifts of life: to authentically share your raw human experience with another being. Being vulnerable allows you to truly feel seen. You still want to choose wisely whom you share with because not everyone earns the right to get to know you more intimately. But when you find the people who love and appreciate you for you and allow yourself to be vulnerable with them, you experience a new kind of love and connection. If you never allow yourself to try this, you miss out on beautiful opportunities.

Healthy and Unhealthy Relationship Dynamics

I generally do not like to label relationships (with friends, coworkers, family, etc.) as "healthy" or "unhealthy." Instead, I prefer to refer to specific patterns in a relationship as healthy or unhealthy. It is sometimes fitting to call an entire relationship unhealthy (or even toxic), when nearly every dynamic is damaging to one or both parties. This is true for relationships that include violence, for example. For the most part, however, it is not up to me or someone else to judge the quality of your relationship. It is much more effective to assess the dynamics within the relationship to point out what can be improved and what is working well.

The best starting point is to understand and identify the components of a relationship that are healthy or unhealthy. These can apply to all types of relationships (friends, romantic partners, family members, coworkers, etc.). Here are some guidelines for healthy relationship dynamics to consider:

- You each respect personal rights (as described in Chapter 5).
- You each take responsibility for yourselves (your actions, opinions, etc.).
- You respect each other's autonomy.
- You respect each other's boundaries.
- You accept and embrace each other as is. You each might have hopes for growth or improvement, but you accept each other where you are right now.
- You support and celebrate each other.
- You communicate with one another.
- You are both mutually open to negotiating to meet each other's needs and wants.
- You each extend grace and compassion when the other makes mistakes.
- You each work toward repairing the relationship if it is injured.
- You reflect each other's value as individual people.

- You support each other when one lacks an ability.
- You act with integrity (through honesty, reliability, etc.)

Dynamics that are generally unhealthy or ineffective include:

- Anything that jeopardizes the safety of one or both parties in the relationship. (If you feel unsafe in a relationship, please ask for support sooner rather than later. A great place to start is to contact the National Domestic Violence Hotline at 800-799-7233.)
- Either of you attempt to exercise power or control over the other.
- Either of you disrespect the other's personal rights.
- Either of you demean or discredit the other's worth.
- Either of you engage in a pattern of dishonesty.
- Both of you get stuck in a pattern of pursuer/distancer (in other words, one chases and the other runs away).
- One or both parties lack compassion, understanding, and/or forgiveness.
- One person's needs and wants are consistently prioritized over the other's, including at the cost of the other's needs and wants.
- One or both parties withdraw or stop communicating.
- Either does not work toward repairing injuries in the relationship (either through dismissal or avoidance of the problem).
- One or both parties deny personal responsibility and/or displace blame onto the other.

The better you understand healthy relationship dynamics, the better you can work to seek relationships with these dynamics or build these dynamics into your current relationships. Conversely, the earlier you detect unhealthy relationship dynamics, the sooner you can choose to work through them, shift the nature of the relationship (such as create more distance), or discontinue the relationship. As the driver of your life, you get to decide.

Negotiables and Non-Negotiables

As you begin or continue to own your value and align your actions with standing in your worth, a very important piece to creating positive relationships is to identify which dynamics, values, and characteristics you want or need in your relationships. A helpful process is to identify what you will accept or not accept. I refer to this process as knowing your "negotiables" and "non-negotiables." Non-negotiables are things you are not willing to negotiate either by way of not permitting them to be a part of the relationship or by requiring them to be a part of the relationship. Cheating might be an example of something you won't tolerate. Some people have a hard and fast rule that if their partner is unfaithful, the relationship is over. No exceptions. An example of a non-negotiable describing something you require in the relationship is the inclusion of physical touch. Many consider this to be a necessity in their relationship because it is their love language.

Negotiables are things that can be negotiated, tweaked, or adjusted within the relationship. These are preferences you are willing to budge on. For example, you might be okay with a partner or roommate who is messy when you prefer to be neat. Or you might be open to different communication styles when it comes to resolving conflict. You might prefer to resolve problems immediately, but when your friend tells you they need time to clarify their thoughts and emotions, you might be open to waiting.

Your preferences and needs are going to differ between relationships. For example, what you tolerate with your sibling might not be the same as what you'd accept from a coworker or partner. You have the right to your preferences. Each person who comes into your life will play a different role and have a different purpose. So, continuing the road trip analogy, ask yourself, "What is the purpose of the trip?" If it is just to run an errand, perhaps you will have different expectations or requirements compared to if it is a trip across the country.

Life is all about trial and error to discover what your negotiables and non-negotiables are. It can take time to realize your negotiables and non-negotiables. Everyone has encountered situations in which they originally thought something was non-negotiable (or vice versa) and then discovered they actually felt comfortable budging to some degree. It is okay for you to adjust your preferences over time and through each experience, particularly as you evolve in discovering and aligning your life with your authentic self.

Personal Reflection

What comes to mind as your negotiables and non-negotiables? How do they differ between various people in your life? Make a list in your journal of things that come to mind.

Assessing Flags

Imagine you have just become friends with someone. You tell a family member about something this person did, and they say, "Be careful. That seems like a red flag to me." You would get the gist of what your family member means, right? You know a red flag warns of danger or problems.

When it comes to entering relationships, it benefits you to assess what future behavior people might engage in. "Flags" are the indicators of possible or probable future behavior. Of course, you cannot see into the future, but there is value in paying attention to patterns of behavior that might inform you of potential behavior later down the road.

To assess flags, here is how I categorize them:

- A "green flag" describes behavior that lines up with what you want and deserve in a relationship. These behaviors indicate it is safe to invite the person in closer and have more involvement in your life.

- A "yellow flag" indicates the need for more information to determine if you will want the behavior to continue in a relationship. Context is likely important to consider. You will want to assess whether it happens often, rarely, or if it is a one-off situation. We all exhibit yellow flag behaviors (because we are imperfect), so these behaviors don't necessarily indicate our character.
- An "orange flag" describes a situation or behavior you should pay very close attention to. Often it is a predictor of a future red flag, but it is possible it is a one-off occurrence where context may make the difference. Gathering more information is important.
- A "red flag" is a behavior that completely goes against what you want and deserve in a relationship. Red flags are indicators that someone's behavior is bad for you. You do not need to gather more information to determine if the behavior is damaging to your well-being.

The purpose of identifying flags is to thoroughly assess whether someone will treat you as you deserve and want over time. When you assess the flags, you support yourself in setting up appropriate expectations of the other person because consistency in action is possibly the best predictor of future behavior. Assessing flags is not about being judgmental or deciding if the person is "good" or "bad." It is merely about determining whether or not their behavior aligns with what is best for you. Referring to the property analogy, it is the process of getting better at determining whom you invite onto your property and into your house.

In this part of the chapter, you will read examples of flags to help you understand the concept further. As you read through them, it is important to note you may not agree with the classifications. I might call something a yellow flag, but you may view it differently. This is also true in your personal life. You and others may not assess the same. This is because we all look at things through different lenses, have different access to information, and have different wants, needs, and values. That is okay as long as you are being clear and honest with yourself about what is best for your life.

Desired Quality: Reliability
(the ability to rely on them to follow through on things)

Green Flag Behavior(s)	Your friend always shows up on time. They communicate ahead of time about plans and if they need to reschedule. If they say they will take care of something, they follow through or communicate their status.
Yellow Flag Behavior(s)	Your friend takes a while to take care of something they committed to. Sometimes they forget about something they have committed to. They follow through and do what they say they are going to do on some commitments, but they struggle with consistency, timing, or communication.
Orange Flag Behavior(s)	Your friend often follows through on things such as showing up when plans are made. However, after three months of consistent follow-through, one weekend they don't show up to a planned event. You try to get a hold of them, wondering if they are okay, but they don't respond. You don't hear back from them until Monday, getting a quick text, "Sorry I forgot, and I wasn't able to get back to you. I'll call you later." You need more information about what happened to determine the seriousness of their no-show and limited communication.
Red Flag Behavior(s)	They consistently cancel plans at the last minute. They say they miss you and want to hang out but have canceled six times in the last two months. They consistently do not complete things they committed to.

Desired Relationship Quality: Fidelity (loyalty and faithfulness in a relationship)

Green Flag Behavior(s)	Your new partner has never cheated in a relationship. They are open and honest about past relationships even when asked hard questions.
Yellow Flag Behavior(s)	Your new partner is evasive when talking about past relationships and/or how the relationships ended. When asked directly if they have ever cheated, they say something like, "I don't want to talk about that right now."
Orange Flag Behavior(s)	Your new partner's best friend makes a flippant comment one night while you all are hanging out about that time your new partner cheated. The situation doesn't allow for gathering more information right then, so you have no idea if the best friend is referring to when they were in middle school or if it was in an adult relationship. You need more information to understand the context of the comment.
Red Flag Behavior(s)	Your new partner admits to having had two affairs in their past marriage.

Desired Quality: Does not engage in violent or abusive behaviors.

Green Flag Behavior(s)	Your roommate, whom you have known for more than ten years, has never engaged in violent or abusive behaviors. When they become angry or upset, they verbalize what they are feeling without raising their voice or changing their physical stance.
Yellow Flag Behavior(s)	Every time your roommate gets angry, they yell loudly and clench their fists.
Orange Flag Behavior(s)	You and your roommate get in one argument one evening while you've both been drinking. Your roommate escalates it by punching the wall. You have never seen this type of behavior before from them. You don't know if this is a one-time behavior or if they have escalated to this degree before.

Red Flag Behavior(s)	Your roommate has an active restraining order against them.

Desired Quality: Comfortable with emotional expression

Green Flag Behavior(s)	Your new friend regularly talks about their emotions when they come up. If they do not want to talk about it or don't know what they are feeling, they say so. They come back to you later and talk about it.
Yellow Flag Behavior(s)	Your new friend sometimes talks about their feelings. Sometimes they shut down and say they need space. They explain they are not used to talking about emotions.
Orange Flag Behavior(s)	Your new friend sometimes shares emotions and has open conversations. However, after having your first disagreement, they don't talk to you for a week. You attempt to contact them, but they don't respond to your calls or texts for a week. You don't know the reason yet for the lack of response for one week or if they resort to silent treatment as a pattern.
Red Flag Behavior(s)	Your new friend regularly says, "There is no reason to talk about emotions." They explain that talking about emotions is something "only weak people do." They do not share their emotions, or they deny they are feeling something when there are several indicators of an emotion being expressed.

Personal Responsibility

When someone displays a yellow, orange, or red flag, I am not advocating that you necessarily cut them loose and don't give them a chance to explain or repair a situation. If we cut every person out of our lives who displayed any flag other than green, we wouldn't have any relationships. We are all bound to make mistakes or struggle. The crucial thing is to pay attention to how they take responsibility for their actions. Do they even take responsibility? If they commit to improving something or doing something differently, do they follow through? If someone either consistently avoids taking ownership, displaces blame, or makes promises but doesn't follow through, these are red flags indicating how they will act in the relationship over time.

If after reading this section you reflect and determine some people in your life consistently demonstrate flags other than green, it does not mean you need to immediately exile them. However, it might indicate you need to adjust their access to you, and you may need to work on modifying your boundaries with them.

The Good Intention/Not a Bad Person Trap

I wholeheartedly believe people generally have good intentions with the majority of choices they make. I also believe in the goodness of humanity.

At the same time, avoid getting into the *good intentions/not a bad person trap* like I used to do constantly. This is when you excuse or permit behavior, generally over and over again, because "They mean well" and "They are good people." This trap used to keep me in many negative relationship dynamics because I rationalized, "But they have a good heart and didn't mean to hurt me." It is easy for many people to get caught in this thinking cycle out of a desire to have empathy and permit forgiveness.

Good intention does not negate the impact of someone's behavior.

As an example, you can feel empathy for someone who was emotionally scarred as a child due to constant parental ridicule. You can see their loving heart and desire to be kind toward them. At the same time, if they get triggered in conversation with you and escalate to the point of screaming at you and calling you derogatory names, then their behavior needs to be recognized and addressed. You have the right to set boundaries about someone acting out toward you in this way. If it is a one-off situation (therefore, in the orange flag category), perhaps you choose to work through it. However, if someone shows consistent patterns, then regardless of intention, you have the right to distance yourself.

Multiple Truths at Once

Deciding what works best for you in a relationship does not equate to making a judgment that the other person is bad, less than, or undeserving of empathy and compassion. It simply means their behavior does not work well for you. You can reconcile this by learning that you can hold more than one opinion at a time regarding someone's behavior. In other words, multiple things can be true at once. For example, you can believe and recognize someone has good intentions behind their behavior, *and* you can determine you do not want to tolerate their behavior. Or, you can feel compassion for why people do what they do *and* set boundaries. Or, you can love someone *and* decide to distance yourself.

Personal Reflection

Reflect on the relationships you have been in or are in. Identify who in your life has consistently demonstrated green flags. Then compare their behavior to those who have displayed yellow, orange, or red flags. Notice if you can find any patterns that are important to remember when choosing new people to bring into your life.

Effective Communication

Alongside your responsibility to determine who you want to allow in is the task of consciously working on how you interact in your relationships.

Healthy interaction almost always depends on one thing: Effective communication. As you master communication, you elevate your relationships.

The Chain of Communication

The first communication tool is what I call the Chain of Communication. I learned this general framework many years ago, but I cannot remember from where, so I cannot give proper credit. However, once I learned it, it stuck with me forever. I have modified the concept somewhat over the years, but communication between two people effectively comes down to these four steps:

1. What person A means inside their head. This includes thoughts, emotions, and experiences.
2. What person A communicates to person B through words, nonverbals, and behaviors.
3. What person B sees, hears, and feels.
4. What person B interprets from person A's communication (how person B makes meaning of what person A communicates).

The goal of all communication is for information to get accurately passed from person A to person B. In other words, A's intended message matches B's understanding. The challenge is there are hundreds of points in this process where understanding can break down. Think of the classic game of telephone. Rarely does the starting phrase make it to the last person exactly as it originated. And this game doesn't even include the translation of nonverbal communication.

When there is a breakdown at any point in the chain of communication, either or both parties are more likely to feel unheard, misunderstood, invalidated, or even judged. As a result, their connection is negatively impacted.

If you keep these steps in mind when you experience a conflict or communication breakdown, you can seek to identify exactly where the breakdown happened. I will provide examples of how to do this later in the chapter.

Communication Styles

Keeping the chain of communication in mind, the next piece to understand is the style in which people generally communicate. Communication style is how people deliver their messages to others. These styles include passive, aggressive, passive-aggressive, and assertive. You have likely heard these terms, but many people do not fully understand what they mean or entail, so I believe it is important to break them down. Read through each of these communication styles to explore and understand your own communication styles.

Passive Communication

Your communication is focused on accommodating others. Your underlying intention is to take care of others before or instead of yourself. You refrain from sharing opinions. You go along with what others want and don't voice what you want. You hold back to avoid potential conflict or discomfort. Your voice might be soft or subdued. Common phrases that indicate passive communication include:

- "Whatever you want works for me."
- "It doesn't matter to me; you choose."
- "I'm fine; nothing is wrong."

For some people, passive communication is accompanied by a quiet or soft voice and/or withdrawn body posture. Often, people whose self-worth has been damaged learn to be passive because they have either internalized that their opinions don't matter or they have experienced life being easier or safer by accommodating others over themselves.

Aggressive Communication

Your communication gives off an impression of being aggressive or overbearing. The underlying intention is to prioritize yourself over others, often disregarding how others might feel or not caring about the effect of your impact on others. Aggressive communication can include displaying a domineering stance (such as hovering above someone) or including physical actions that communicate potential threat to safety (such as throwing something across the room). Your voice might be loud, to the point of yelling or screaming.

Passive-Aggressive Communication

Passive-aggressive communication is possibly the most common communication style and occurs when your spoken words state one thing and your other communication cues (voice, tone, body language, etc.) say another. Through your words, you verbalize that you are prioritizing the other person, but internally, you prioritize yourself. The best way to identify if you are being passive-aggressive is if you are expressing one message through your words, but internally, you are feeling or thinking something else and are revealing some kind of indication of this internal experience through your non-verbal communication. As a result, the person on the other end of the interaction is confused about what you are thinking or feeling.

Many people think that passive-aggressiveness means displaying aggressive behavior, which is understandable because it has the word in the name. However, passive-aggressive communication is pretty much any communication that sends conflicting messages. Examples include:

- You answer, "I'm fine," when someone asks you if you are okay, but you won't make eye contact with them and your body language is slumped, sending the message that you are not fine.
- You say, "It's not a problem," but you are shutting the kitchen cabinets with more energy or force than normal.

- When someone asks your opinion of what to do, you answer, "Do whatever you want. It doesn't matter to me," as you roll your eyes and then walk out of the room.
- You give someone the silent treatment. Silence by itself is just being quiet. The silent treatment is ignoring with the underlying intention of showing the other person you are upset and consciously choosing to ignore them.

At this point in the book, I wish I could insert a recording of myself using passive-aggressive communication. Because I was a pro! Passive-aggressiveness was my main mode of communication until my thirties because it was one way I learned to get some of my needs met.

As embarrassing as it is for me to say, and possibly embarrassing for you to admit as well, often when we are using passive-aggressive communication, we are trying to elicit a feeling or action in someone else. We are trying to poke at them so they will eventually meet our needs. Have you heard how people joke that you have to ask a woman four times if she is really okay before she will tell you? Many women laugh when they hear this (like I did the first time) because we can relate. When I was younger and answered, "I'm fine," I said the words, but I made it known through my voice and/or body language that I was not actually fine. People do this because something stops them from feeling that it is okay to provide the honest answer, such as "I'm mad" or "I've had an awful day." Can you see when this has been true for you?

I was constantly passive-aggressive until one of my closest friends started directly calling me out on it. She made it clear she wasn't going to enable the behavior or cater to me when I was being indirect. She told me point blank she was not going to guess what I was thinking or feeling, declaring that I had to take ownership, not her. This calling out was one of the best gifts I have ever received because it prompted me to truly shift how I showed up for myself and in relationships.

Mitigating this behavior requires you to go through a process of being honest with yourself about whether you are, in fact, trying to elicit a response from someone or if something is preventing you from being direct.

Assertive Communication

Assertive communication is the act of aligning all parts of your communication so you send a clear message that matches what you mean. Your words and nonverbal cues are completely congruent. The receiver does not have to guess what you are saying or meaning because you are clear. When you communicate, you are honoring both yourself and the other person.

Assertive communication is the goal. Mean what you say through both your words and actions while holding respect for yourself and the person on the receiving end.

If you have not been taught or encouraged to communicate assertively, I understand the difficult learning curve. It will be a process, but shifting the way you communicate is completely doable and will reap tremendous benefits.

Guidelines for Becoming More Assertive

1. Learn to identify each communication style used by others. Observe people you know and people you don't know. Ask yourself the following questions:

    - Do their words and nonverbals appear to communicate one message or meaning?
    - Do you feel you need to guess what they are really thinking or meaning? If so, why? If not, why?
    - When they communicate, whose needs do they seem to be concerned with (only themselves, only others, or both)?

2. Get to know your own communication style. Use the questions below to get to know yourself:

    - Did I say what I really meant or wanted to say?
    - When I communicated, did my choice of words, the sound of my words, and my body language all communicate the same message?
    - How and with whom do my communication styles change?

3. Identify the factors that get in the way of communicating assertively. Reflect on these questions:

    - When I communicate, what stops me from saying what I really feel or think? (This often stems from fearing something or wanting to avoid something.)
    - Which elements of my communications send a conflicting message to others?
    - How am I trying to get my own needs or desires met through my communication?
    - Am I being clear about what I want or need?
    - Am I honoring what someone else wants?
    - Am I taking responsibility only for myself, attempting to take responsibility for others, or pushing them to take responsibility for me?
    - How could I communicate differently if given another chance?

4. Identify what helps you communicate assertively.

    - Name situations or people with whom you are completely honest when you communicate.

- Identify what supports you in feeling comfortable to assert yourself.

5. Increase your assertive communication one interaction at a time.

   - Determine when and with whom you want to become more assertive.
   - Before communicating, identify to yourself exactly what you mean. Identify the emotion you are feeling if that is something you need to express. Identify the thought(s) in your mind. If it is an emotionally charged situation, take time to do this on your own through writing so you can get all of it out and sort through it before you have a conversation.
   - Determine the words you will use and the nonverbal cues you will display that match what you genuinely mean.
   - Start practicing with the people who foster a sense of safety and support for you. Let them know you are trying to improve your assertive communication skills and will be practicing to make sure your words and nonverbal communication match what you mean.

Personal Reflection

Make a list of people you feel you can always communicate honestly with. Then identify what it is about them or your relationship that creates this sense of comfort and safety. Next, make a list of people you hold back from and, therefore, become more passive with. What is it about them or the dynamics that prompts you to hold back? Last, make a list of people with whom you have used aggressive or passive-aggressive communication. What dynamics are at play with those people? What gets in the way of staying centered and/or being direct and honest?

Growth Activity

One way to gain a deeper understanding of the different types of communication is to observe other people. Think of some place you might go where you can discretely observe how others interact. Take notice of their verbal and nonverbal communication. Notice how well their words match their nonverbal cues. If you can't find a place you feel comfortable doing this live, you can always watch a movie or TV show to do this activity.

Balancing Honesty and Respect

One of the most common questions I get from people is, "How do I communicate assertively if I don't want to tell them what I am thinking or feeling?" The biggest reasons people don't want to share include:

- They fear hurting feelings.
- They don't think they know how to say things nicely.
- They do not feel safe with or trust the person to not react negatively.
- They do not feel like sharing.

Each of these reasons is completely valid. You are not obligated to share with others. You have the right to choose with whom you share. And you have the responsibility to maintain respect when you share. Therefore, situations can be very tricky when learning to be assertive.

My answer always comes back to: Start with being honest with yourself (what you are genuinely thinking or feeling) and then determine which details you want to communicate. You do not have to choose between sharing nothing and sharing everything. You can express something in between. Imagine a coworker asks, "How is your day going?" You think to yourself, *This day has been really crappy because our boss is being really difficult, but I can't share this because it would be unprofessional.* To answer honestly while not divulging too much information, you can say, "Eh, I've had some challenges today, but I'm getting through them." With this type of answer, you are naming the fact that your day has included challenges and you are naming that you are getting through them.

You also always have the right to say you don't want to talk about something. You are not obligated to share anything you don't want to or talk when you don't want to. This might look like you attending a family function and your cousin asks, "How are you and your boyfriend doing? The last time we saw each other, you two got into an argument." You are thinking to yourself, *I have no idea. We keep getting in fights, and I am not sure if we are good for each other. I also suspect he is cheating on me.* But you don't divulge all while at the family function and as your boyfriend sits ten feet away. You can reply, "I don't really feel like talking about it right now. I appreciate you asking and checking up on me, though."

Cultural Considerations

It is important not to confuse these communication styles with cultural norms that are a part of your life and that you feel comfortable with. For example, if you live in a culture that uses loud volume when communicating, that does not mean you all are being aggressive. It just means you all speak louder. Aggressive communication is about the person bulldozing another person's rights, wants, and needs. If you and all your siblings feel comfortable screaming at each other for a while to work through something, but you are each holding a level of respect and compassion underneath, then go for it.

In another respect, if you live in a culture that prioritizes certain people's voices over others, and you are aware of this, you may consciously choose not to disrupt the system by inserting your own voice. Sometimes you might just choose to be passive because it fits best with your cultural norms. It is okay to do this *when* you are consciously choosing to because you are weighing all the factors at play. For example, maybe you don't feel like hashing out political issues with your ninety-two-year-old grandfather who grew up in a completely different era because you would rather spend your time with him playing cards and connecting. Consciously choosing to honor your cultural norms is different from avoiding and denying your authentic self.

Ask and Clarify

I used to feel absolutely destroyed when receiving certain (constructive) feedback or when someone seemed upset with me. That is because I took what they said (both verbally and nonverbally) and assigned an inaccurate meaning to it. For example, if someone said, "I was kind of frustrated the other day when you wouldn't give me a straight answer about what you wanted to do," I might have theorized what they really meant was I was a bad person for not expressing myself. I created a meaning the person hadn't actually expressed.

Everyone infers meaning. It is part of the blessing and the curse of being human and having the ability to deduce information without having all the facts. But know that sometimes when you do this, it can cause damage or conflict if what you infer is inaccurate. The most powerful solution to prevent such breakdowns is: Clarify. Clarify. Clarify.

If you, at any point, are unsure of what someone means because you are confused by what they are communicating, then ask them to clarify. Invite them to explain more so you understand better. Or explain how you are personally interpreting what they are saying. Here are some powerful ways to ask for clarity in a respectful and assertive way:

- "I'm not sure I understand what you mean. Can you explain more?"
- "I feel confused about whether you are upset right now because you said you weren't when I asked, and then you went to the bedroom and closed the door without saying anything else."
- "When you said you are tired of always having to do the dishes, I took it to mean you don't feel like I do them often enough. Is that what you feel?"
- "What do you want from me or hope I will do instead?"

I guarantee if you increase your awareness of how you ascribe meaning to what other people communicate and combine that with taking the time to clarify what they mean, you will have fewer communication breakdowns. This means fewer conflicts, hurt feelings, anxiety, and disconnection. When you have a fuller understanding of what others mean, you get to rest easier and take their word rather than spending time in your head coming up with problematic scenarios that only increase your anxiety and decrease feelings of worthiness.

Healthy Relationships Heal Wounds

A ton of evidence indicates emotional injuries caused by other people can have lasting effects on us. I don't even need to bring in academic research to make this point because I am sure you can think of at least one relationship that negatively affected you.

Conversely, there is also overwhelming evidence that we can heal our core wounds and sense of belonging by being in relationships with others. Dr. Sue Johnson, a relationship expert I highly respect, proclaims: "creating connection is our most ancient survival code."[2] When you invite into your life people who truly see you, respect you, and treat you with love and kindness, you can more fully heal your relationship with yourself and the painful parts of your history. You have the capacity to create a reciprocal exchange by inviting in people who treat you well and setting the standards for how your relationships function. It's a two-way street between the standards you set for how you are treated and the standards you live by in how you treat others. The better you communicate with others, the better people will communicate with you. The clearer boundaries you set, the more people will respect your boundaries. The more authentic and honest you are with yourself, the more you will attract authentic people. You will then worry less about not being good enough because they will reflect your worth.

2 https://drsuejohnson.com. Accessed March 11, 2023.

As you practice and refine how you relate to others, your choices as to whom you invite into your life will become clearer. The choices you make from this point forward, as you will learn in the next chapter, are yours. It is up to you to ensure people earn their right to be in your life based on how they honor your worth. You will be drawn toward the ease and joy that builds when you connect with those people.

CHAPTER 7
Integrating the Power of Choice

"Sometimes the smallest step in the right direction ends up being the biggest step of your life. Tiptoe if you must, but take the step."

— Naeem Callaway

I understand what it is like to feel powerless. I know how it feels not to believe or trust that things will get better or easier.

I also know life constantly includes the choice to keep moving forward.

You always have choices. You may not have access to the same choices as the person next to you. But, at each and every moment, you have choices to put one foot in front of the other. When you learn to recognize, understand, and own your choices, you empower yourself to create the life of your dreams.

Discovering My Truth

After I took the spring semester off in 2000, I returned to Vanderbilt in July to complete a summer course and then begin my senior year. I ran into a friend as I was walking across campus. We were happy to see each other, and I knew he was glad I was doing better—he knew why I had been gone the previous semester.

At some point in our conversation, I said my recovery included psychotherapy and antidepressant medication. He said, "I don't believe in medication or therapy. Happiness is a choice. You can choose to be happy."

Poof. All of the wind left my sail.

I had just spent an intense eight months learning about my illnesses and tirelessly working to improve my mental state through medication and therapy, all to essentially be told the tools I used were a crock of shit. The meaning I initially took from his statement: I'm at fault for my sadness because I was not *choosing* to be happy.

I began the walk back to my dorm feeling deflated. After about ten minutes, however, I began to tap back into my truth.

The first truth I recognized was this friend did genuinely care about me and did not mean anything negative. I knew his statement came from a naive place—he knew nothing about mental health. (Remember, at the time it was less common and much more stigmatized for someone to get mental health treatment.) I recognized that because he had not experienced anything similar, he could not possibly understand my experience.

The second truth I acknowledged was I was not at fault for my struggles. I did not choose for significant life events to change me so profoundly starting at two years old. I did not choose for my brain and body to be impaired by depression, anxiety, or trauma. I did not consciously choose to start hating myself as a child. I also knew I had tried my hardest to will my way to happiness, but that my brain lacked the chemicals to feel better.

And last but not least, the third truth I recognized as I recentered was: He was partially correct in that I did have choices. I had the choice to work toward stabilizing my mental health, and I was actively making that choice every day. I did choose to get help and find support. I was choosing to learn about and use tools to better my life every day. Most importantly, I made the choice every day to keep going even when some days all I could do was choose to live.

I am most proud of this one choice: I chose to believe in my dream of graduating from Vanderbilt and becoming a mental health professional. Even though I returned to school still struggling with feeling less than worthy and not good enough, compounded by the rejection of several friends, I chose to believe in my dream. And that is how I got to where I am today.

The Power of Choice

For a few months during the process of writing this book, I agonized over whether I should include this chapter. Mostly, I hesitated because I feared my message would get misconstrued as supporting toxic positivity or buying into damaging belief systems about equality.

I want to be clear from the get-go: I do not support, "It's simple; just choose to [blank]" or "Everyone can do [blank] with their lives if they really want to." Because the reality is that some things are not just a matter of choice. Not all people have equal access to certain choices. And not all things just happen in the blink of an eye because one just *chooses* it. Therefore, I am not telling you that everything lies on your shoulders to make something happen right here and now.

What I do stand by: Each day you are presented with moment-to-moment choices that can lead to important shifts in your life.

Understanding that you have the power to choose is a vital tool for the process of embodying your worth and creating the life you want. As I increased awareness of my choices and increased personal responsibility for the everyday actions related to this growth, my life shifted drastically. I began to consciously ask myself questions such as, "Do I want to act passive-aggressively right now to get my needs met, or will I be direct about my needs?" or "Do I prefer to invest in this relationship that injures my self-esteem, or am I going to learn how to let go so I can invest my energy elsewhere?"

Have you ever played chess? I have never learned how, but I know each move a player makes is based on strategy. Someone who knows how to play chess knows what each piece symbolizes and the rules associated with each. If I were to play, I would just be randomly moving the pieces. Because the board looks like a checkerboard, I would assume I was just trying to get to the other side of the board. If I played with someone who knows the rules, I would inevitably lose. The person who knows how to play would be thinking through every move they make and several moves into the future.

Your choices are similar. If you come at life blindly by just acting on autopilot at every turn, you are bound to run into more trouble than if you think thoroughly through things. That doesn't mean you won't run into millions of things outside your control. But you empower yourself by learning how you respond at each step of your journey in a way that moves you in the direction you desire.

Conscious Choosing

Think about how much of your life is run on autopilot. When your alarm goes off, you get up and start your morning routine. When you get into a heated discussion with a close relative, you start communicating differently with them compared to other people in your life.

Even though you operate on autopilot much of the time, I estimate you engage in thousands of decisions each day. You just aren't fully aware you are making choices because so many of them have become instinctual.

In some moments throughout the day, it might be more obvious you are selecting between options. Some of those choices might seem pretty inconsequential. For example, you might ask yourself quickly, "Should I go to the bathroom now or when we get to the restaurant?" or "Should I start at the produce section or the other side of the store today?" You recognize you are presented with possibilities, you weigh the options, and you move forward with a decision.

Other choices might have a glaringly obvious decision-making process. This could include something like deciding to change jobs. In the process, you will likely know your potential options. You might make a list of pros and cons, staying at your current job versus accepting a job elsewhere. You are actively and consciously engaging in making a decision that is right for you.

A key to building the life of your dreams is elevating your consciousness of the choices available to you and the potential outcomes of those choices. I call this *conscious choosing*. When you raise your awareness of the available choices and what to consider with each choice, you live from an empowered position rather than being powerless. You learn to proactively decide which moves to make to get to your desired path. Conscious choosing is the direct way to take ownership and responsibility of your life, moment to moment. It takes you off autopilot so you are not only driving your journey, but determining the route to your destination.

Conscious Choosing Process

The process of making conscious and strategic choices can be simple. If you are thinking about moving, you will compare different places based on price, location, and personal needs. The factors may be more concrete; therefore, it is easier to outline your choices and make a decision.

When it comes to personal growth and healing, however, the process is less straightforward. Throughout my history of healing myself and helping clients heal, I have found the following guidelines to be most helpful in making powerful and growth-oriented decisions.

Defining Your Goal

Elevating your consciousness about your choices begins with deciding what you want to accomplish. Therefore, with each choice you make, explore these questions:

1. What do I want to achieve?
2. How do I want to feel?

3. What do I want to believe about myself?
4. What do I want to happen in the near future (short-term)?
5. What outcomes am I hoping for long-term?

Frank has really felt work burnout for the past few months. His wife suggests he look for a new job. He is conflicted. He has been working at his company for eighteen years. He knows all the ins and outs of his job. He used to really enjoy his duties until he got a new manager last summer who works at least seventy hours a week and expects everyone else to work the same hours because they are "salary." The previous manager stressed and modeled work-life balance. Frank is not totally clear about what he wants, but he knows he doesn't want to, nor can he, keep up with the current expectations because it is leading him to feel like not showing up at all.

Sometimes you may be unclear about what you *want*, but you can identify what you *don't* want. It is okay to start by naming what you don't want. Once you define what you are not going for, identify the opposite of that. The opposite likely identifies what you do want. In the example above, Frank knows he doesn't want to work seventy hours a week because he feels exhausted when he does. So he then works backward to determine that he wants to feel energized and that a work week of an average of forty hours is best for him. Another example is perhaps you personally no longer want to feel lonely. You think of what is the opposite of lonely and identify it as connected. Therefore, you realize you desire to find ways to feel more connected with others.

Sometimes you may desire outcomes that seem to be in opposition to each other. For example, while you want to feel more connected, you also want to ensure you have enough alone-time to recharge your energy. When you have seemingly competing goals, name each of them and give yourself permission to want more than one thing at once. This opens up your lens to seek solutions that meet each goal. If a solution cannot satisfy all goals, you will weigh which one is most important at the time and own that you are prioritizing one goal over another.

Weighing Your Options

Take time to explore your options when making decisions. Ask yourself these questions in the process:

1. What choices are realistically available to me now?
2. What steps go into each option?
3. What possible outcomes come with each option? (*Possible* means anything that could theoretically happen.)
4. What probable outcomes come with each option? (*Probable* means likely.)
5. Why do I want to choose each option?
6. Why do I not want to choose each option?

Jonas is freaking out. He just got notice that his roommate of three years plans to move in with his partner when their lease is up in a few months. Jonas supports his roommate while feeling overwhelmed at the thought of moving. He has all sort of questions: Who will I live with? Can I afford to live on my own? Which part of town can I afford? Should I buy instead of rent? *Jonas decides to make a list of his possible options. He takes a deep breath and reminds himself he can spend the next couple of weeks researching options, particularly in regard to the housing and rental markets. He knows once he has more facts about his options, he will be able to discover what is optimal for him at this time.*

Something to understand from the get-go with looking at all your options is: Information is power. While I did not come up with this phrase, I will repeat it until I am blue in the face because the more information you have, the more you empower yourself to make the best decisions for you. The more you know about what is included with each option, the better you will feel with the choices you make. I watch people freeze in their decision-making process all the time because they spend their time guessing what the options entail rather than investigating. Therefore, take the time to gather information. If you are toying with the idea of relocating to a new city to potentially improve your life, research the city. If you hesitate to change jobs because you fear something else won't pay as much, look at job advertisements and compare salary ranges. Rather than keeping "what ifs" in your mind, investigate. It doesn't mean you are committing. It just means you are assessing your options.

As you think through options, be realistic. I like to think of this in terms of probability based on previous evidence. For example, if you are thinking about how you are going to address your boss about your workload, reflect on all the possible ways they could respond. Then identify what is more likely to happen based on previous evidence. I think of all the times I feared (and predicted) someone had randomly decided to no longer be my friend because they hadn't called me back. Was it possible? Yes, because pretty much anything is possible. But was it probable based on history? No.

When you are thinking through your potential choices, recognize that *not* acting is also a choice you can make. Name the potential outcomes of not doing something, and if you decide you prefer those outcomes over acting, it is perfectly okay to not act.

Evie works in an office full of cubicles. She has a new officemate who taps the desk while on hold during calls. Evie finds this somewhat distracting when trying to read through documents. Evie contemplates bringing this to the officemate's attention. She decides that she does not yet feel comfortable addressing it because she does not know her coworker well enough to know how she might respond. She opts to wait until she builds a better relationship with the coworker. In the meantime, she recognizes that it will continue to be distracting, so she starts bringing headphones.

Embrace Your Current Self

It is extremely common to get down on yourself for not "being able to" make certain choices now. This is often tied to having feelings of regret or shame about past events related to your current situation. I often hear about this in terms of "because I did [blank] before, I can't [blank] now." Well, you cannot change the past, and you cannot fast-forward time. So, with each choice you make, meet yourself where you are now.

Give yourself understanding, grace, and compassion for your current status. Validate your existing capabilities rather than pressuring yourself to be somewhere else or "further along." Know that not having some choices yet available to you is not a reflection on who you are or a judgment of you. It also doesn't mean they definitely won't be available to you in the future. Highlight your current options that can lead you toward your bigger goals.

Lily got in an argument with her sister last weekend. Her sister has a pattern of giving Lily the silent treatment when they have a conflict. They are supposed to see each other at an upcoming family function, and the thought of getting the silent treatment again makes Lily's stomach sink. She has been learning that she needs to set boundaries with people, so she knows she should have a conversation with her sister soon. But Lily just isn't ready right now because she has a major exam coming up and needs to focus on studying. Lily chooses not to address the issue before the family function while fully acknowledging she will feel uncomfortable at the family event without having resolved the situation.

Repeat the following truths to yourself:

1. I am making this choice based on where I am now.
2. This choice does not mean I won't have new choices in the future.
3. I cannot fast-forward time. All I can do is be in this moment.
4. I am in the process of (learning, growing, adjusting, etc.).
5. I am not there yet; I am working toward getting there.
6. Where I am today is not a reflection of *who* I am. It is merely a fact of the present time.

Own Your Decisions

Once you have explored your options, claim your decision and take responsibility for all that comes with it. As I like to say: Own it.

If you have decided to get back together with your ex based on weighing all factors, okay. Own it. Own that you are taking a risk. Own that you have weighed the pros and cons to the best of your ability. Own that you are consciously choosing to engage in the relationship. Own how you are consciously choosing to engage in it differently this time.

If you decide not to confront someone because you anticipate they will ridicule you, and you just don't feel you have the bandwidth to deal with the ridicule, okay. Own it. Own that you are preserving your energy. Own that you do not want to deal with the experience of being ridiculed.

If you are on the fence about something, such as looking for and applying for a new job, and you decide to wait, okay. Own it. Own that you see how getting a different job could be good for you. Own that you also like the stability and sense of safety with the current job.

When you consciously and confidently own your choices, you will feel liberated, more in control, and empowered. So, with each conscious choice you make, claim, "Yes! I choose this for myself at this moment."

Pitfalls to Avoid

People may encounter some pitfalls when growing toward taking increased ownership of personal choice.

Pitfall One: Believing "I have no choice but to...."

Truth: You have more than one option. The other options may be unattractive or extremely difficult. But you have more than one option. Sometimes you might be too close to a situation to feel or believe you have more than one option. Sometimes the "other" option(s) may be so clearly wrong you believe you don't have an option. But the reality is: the *wrong* thing is also an option.

I think of the multiple conversations I have had with parents that go something like this:

> Parent: Well, of course, I provided for them [their child]; I didn't have a choice.
>
> Me: Yes, you did have a choice. You had the option to take care of them and the option not to. You had the option to work hard to provide a roof over their head and the option to use drugs and not hold down a job.
>
> Parent: Well, of course, I took care of them.
>
> Me: Not of course, because plenty of people don't make this same choice. You did.

Another statement I hear from people is, "Well, I couldn't just let them suffer. I had to help." Actually, you *can* let people deal with life challenges themselves. You have the option not to get involved. However, you choose to involve yourself because you value compassion and being helpful. Not all people choose to help, and it's worth praising and recognizing yourself for living in alignment with your values.

When you ignore having choices, you shortchange yourself by not seeing your power. You also miss out on recognizing your strengths. When you recognize your choices and what you are intentionally *not* choosing, this opens up so much more room to have confidence in why you choose what you choose. You learn to recognize and acknowledge how you are proactive.

If you notice that you see yourself as having no choice in a situation, take some time to reflect on the validity of this statement. If it helps you, recall how others have responded differently in similar situations. From there, you can identify what went into or is going into your decision-making process. Name what you are prioritizing among the range of choices available.

Pitfall Two: Believing something will never happen, so you give up.

Truth: You might think to yourself, *I could never do that* or *I will never have that.* Yes, some things may not be possible right now. Some things may seem impossible. At the same time, you do not know if something will be impossible forever. You don't *actually* know what the future holds. You don't know what opportunities might come your way. You don't know what skills you may learn along the way that could lead you to achieving that *impossible* dream.

Right now, smaller steps are available to you that have the potential to lead you to your desired outcome. You can identify what is unrealistic now, and you can name what might be improbable. And you can break your goals down into much smaller chunks to create building blocks toward your bigger goal. When you continue to build on your building blocks, you potentially create a future you never imagined. If you align your actions with the belief that your long-term goal isn't attainable, then you don't act and you set yourself up to miss out on what might have been.

If you run into this thought process or feel powerless, break down your long-term goal into smaller steps. From those steps, determine if you can accomplish some forward movement.

Pitfall Three: Confusing victimization with playing victim.

Truth: If you have been on the receiving end of mistreatment, abuse, oppression, or violence, you have been victimized. You have also survived the victimization, thus the term survivor. However, you are not by definition "a victim." Your victimization does not define you as a person. It is something that has happened to you; it is not *who* you are.

The most common worry I hear from clients when they have been victimized is, "But I don't want to act like a victim and make excuses for why I did what I did."

If you choose to name your experience for what it was and seek to understand how those events influenced your life, then you are not "playing victim." Playing victim is believing you are powerless and have no responsibility for what happens next. If you are choosing to express your emotions and talk about your experience, that is the complete opposite of acting powerless or irresponsible. It is owning what happened and that your life was affected by it. Talking about your experiences can be a very important step in healing and growing to reach a greater awareness of your current choices.

Pitfall Four: Trying to BS yourself into believing something is a good option or something you want when you know deep down it's not.

Truth: You can't bullshit yourself. More specifically, your mind can try to bullshit its way into making a decision, but you can't bullshit your *true self.*

We humans are really good at convincing ourselves that a choice is okay or good even if we know there will likely be negative consequences. Where are all my peeps who have said, "I'll be fine hanging out with my ex… at their house…to watch a movie…."? Do I need to finish the rest of the story? You and I both know the situation. Your best friends say, "Don't do it," and you assure them, "We are just friends now. I'm totally over them." How much time did you spend convincing yourself and others that this time would be different, but you knew deep down how the evening would play out?

Another example is suppose I am working with my health coach or doctor, and they say I need to start waking up at six each morning because it is good for me. And I reply, "I know, so I will start tomorrow." I decide to commit because I feel like I *should.* The reality: I know myself. I am not going to adjust my entire lifestyle to wake up that early every day. I have a condition that inhibits my ability to get restorative sleep, so I have zero evidence indicating I can be successful with that schedule long-term, *and* I just don't like being up that early. One of my greatest joys is sleeping in.

I could commit to one or two days a week; that would be feasible. But not every day.

Here's the deal. Your life choices improve when you are truthful with yourself. Be honest about what is really at play with your choices and their potential outcomes. Taking the example above, admit that part of you wishes your ex wanted you back. Or that part of you wants to just live in the moment, grabbing some short-term gratification and forgetting about the consequences. It's okay to admit these things because you are human. Just prepare yourself for the probable outcomes of your choices and how you plan to deal with them. Owning what is realistic is far better than spinning your wheels pretending or pushing yourself to be someone you are not.

When you plan your steps around who you really are, what you really want, and how you really operate, you will find solutions that fit you best. You will set yourself up for success. You will also set yourself up for others to appreciate you as you are now, not how they imagined you to be.

The Fuck-Its

You know those times when you know full-well that what you are about to do is going to come with consequences, but you say "Fuck it. I'm doing it anyway!"

For example, you go out to a bar with your friends on a work night. You know you need to get up early in the morning, but you are having fun and the drinks are flowing. You think about being hungover the next day, but you ultimately decide, "What does it matter? I'm having fun!" So, you continue drinking despite how you might feel the next day at work. You essentially say, "Fuck It!" to making the "responsible" choice.

This is what I call the "Fuck-Its."

We all have fuck-it moments. And that is perfectly okay, as long as you are completely honest with yourself about what you are choosing and the consequences of your fuck-it choices.

If You Don't Go, You Don't Get

My dad, Bob, taught me early, "If you don't go, you don't get," based on a plaque he has on his desk:

"If I don't go, I don't get."

In the South is an old man with a rowboat
who ferries passengers across a mile-wide river for ten cents.

Asked, "How many times a day do you do this?" he said,
"As many times as I can because the more I go, the more I get.
And if I don't go, I don't get."

Bob and my mom beautifully instilled in me that the best I can do for myself is put one foot in front of the other and try. They taught me that taking steps toward where I want to go is better than not moving at all, because when you don't at least try, you miss out on the possibilities and opportunities for your life to improve (in whatever way you define).

The more you can recognize your choices, the more you will recognize your capabilities. As a result, you will learn to do things from an empowered place. You will learn to take more chances. You will learn that success is attainable. You will learn that you are okay if things don't go the way you originally planned. You will learn that even when you don't have control of something, you have control of how you show up in those moments. When you own how you choose to be in each moment, you learn to love yourself more fully for doing your best.

I invite you, right now, to choose yourself. Choose to keep learning to love yourself and act to honor this love. Do this by planning how you will move forward, even if by tiptoeing, as the quote says at the beginning of the chapter. Hold this commitment in mind as you imagine your growth and healing toolbox, which you will explore in the next chapter.

Growth Activity

When you picked up this book, you created the goal of embodying your worth to build the life you want. Now that you have read through all the tools and concepts, put a plan in action. Begin by brainstorming the goals you want to achieve to support your self-worth journey. List the new choices you will work toward making that reflect embodying your worth. Name how you will align your behavior with "I am valuable, beyond worthy, and deserve good things." Then use some kind of art form (markers, paint, etc.) to illustrate your "Self-Worth Strategy Map" based on what you brainstorm. Use your creativity to visualize what this will look like for you throughout the next year.

CHAPTER 8
Expanding Your Wellness Toolbox

"The secret of change is to focus all your energy not on fighting the old, but on building the new."

— Dan Millman

Do We Ever Arrive?

When I was a teenager, I had this very clear vision: "When I am twenty-five, I will finally be able to have the relationship I want with my dad (Lee)." I predicted I would be able to go see him when I wanted. I would have money to call him when I wanted. I imagined I wouldn't have to wait around for him, but instead I could go to him. I would have control of the situation. I also anticipated I would be more mature. With that maturity, I predicted I would be healed and no longer "broken." I don't even know where I got the age twenty-five from, but it was clear as day to me that my life would be completely different by then.

Curiously, I know I am not the only one who expected everything to fall into place by twenty-five, or at the latest by thirty, because I have heard this expectation countless times from other twenty-somethings. They would say, "I thought I would be over this by now," or "I'm not normal because I still have these issues going on." I can't exactly pinpoint how so many of us received the message that we are behind in life, but the message is loud and creates a lot of undo shame.

Here is the reality I have learned: None of us are behind because there is no such thing as having "arrived." Instead, life is ever-changing, ever-evolving. We ebb and flow with our challenges. We may improve, but then a new situation will throw a curveball. Healing and growing is a constant process of life.

Your task is to love yourself as you learn to heal and grow during each chapter of your life.

Your Growth and Healing Toolbox

Imagine you want to build a house. You may or may not have instructions, but you know how to find a toolbox that will contain helpful items for construction. At first, maybe you only own a few basic tools, such as a hammer, nails, pliers, and a screwdriver. Over time, as you want to expand what you build, you get exposed to tools you never knew existed.

You are metaphorically building your own house each day. You have your own life toolbox. You were taught certain tools as a child. You have played around with different strategies as you have gotten older. And if you make the choice, you can work on expanding the tools in your toolbox every day from here on out.

I invite you to declare this life toolbox as your Growth and Healing Toolbox. There is no right or wrong on what you add or how you learn to maneuver the tools over time. All tools are welcome because all entry points to healing have value and purpose. Your life projects are always going to be changing. Give yourself grace for practicing the tools, gathering new ones, and learning to tweak the ones you have.

The strategies outlined in this book are valuable additions to your Growth and Healing Toolbox. At the same time, many other tools are out there that I feel are important to know about and potentially explore in your future. Use this chapter to decide which additional tools you want to include in your toolbox to continue your growth and healing journey.

Care for Your Trauma

As you learned in Chapter 1, the body and mind can be heavily impacted by traumatic life events. The effects can be long-term (even to the point of continuing through generations) and can range from mild to severe. A worthwhile action you can take is to learn how trauma affects you personally. When you gain a deeper understanding of trauma, you are likely to feel less alone and more "normal" as a human. Your life will make more sense to you. Here are resources to consider:

- National Institute of Mental Health: https://www.nimh.nih.gov/e (nih.gov)
- National Center for PTSD: https://www.ptsd.va.gov/
- European Society for Traumatic Stress Studies: https://estss.org/
- *The Wisdom of Trauma* movie: https://thewisdomoftrauma.com/
- *What Happened to You* by Bruce D. Perry, MD, PhD, and Oprah Winfrey
- *My Grandmother's Hands* by Resmaa Menakem
- *The Boy Who Was Raised by a Dog* by Bruce D. Perry
- *Embodied Self Awakening* by Nityda Gessel

You can also deepen your healing by getting specific trauma treatment, which you can read more about in the Professional Resources section of this chapter.

Inner Child Work

Imagine you slam your finger in a door today. You go see a doctor to get it treated. The doctor orders an x-ray of your finger and discovers you have a previous injury. When asked about it, you say, "Oh, it's no big deal. It happened years ago when I fell off my bike. I let it heal on its own and it seems to be fine." The doctor then explains that you will need to treat the previous break to be able to fully heal today's fracture, so the doctor puts your finger in a cast.

Many of your self-worth wounds today are connected to childhood. Similar to the fractured finger, healing can be optimal if you work on healing those childhood wounds. You improve yourself by focusing on current challenges. You experience more powerful change by nurturing the child within you who was originally wounded. This is known as inner child work.

When you do inner child work, you get in touch with your innocence. You gain understanding of how your thought patterns, behaviors, and ways of seeing the world were originally created. You learn to nurture the younger versions of your being so your current self can feel loved and cared for. If you weren't given unconditional love as a child, you get the chance to do this for yourself now by doing inner child work.

You can both request a professional to guide you through inner child work or you can search for "Healing the Inner Child" resources online. I personally really appreciate the work of Dr. Somer Nicole who specializes in reparenting the inner child through somatic practices. She is the creator of Somatic Reparenting Method™ and provides resources in a variety of formats. You can see these options through her link tree at: www.linktr.ee/dr_somer_nicole

Self-Compassion Work

Learning how to be compassionate with yourself can take a lot of time and practice, especially if you have a strong inner critic. Many people promote self-compassion work, but Dr. Kristin Neff is revered as the leader in self-compassion work. She has a self-assessment tool on her website www.self-compassion.org that you might find valuable. She has also written books. Many people have told me *The Mindful Self-Compassion Workbook*, written by Dr. Neff and Dr. Germer, was helpful in their healing journey.

Physical Health

We all "know" that taking care of our body is essential to our overall well-being and mental health. At the same time, how many of us don't take care of our bodies in the ways we know we "should"? No matter how difficult it can be to prioritize physical health, it is vital to our mental and emotional well-being. When you integrate proper sleep, nutrition, and exercise, your body is able to reach optimal functioning. This then positively impacts your sense of worth.

I encourage you to experiment with how your body feels in response to being less versus more active, comparing different foods and diets, and refraining from harmful products like alcohol, cigarettes, or drugs. Listen to your body; be curious about what it tells you. Track your energy levels, concentration, etc. If you desire to seek support in this area, I encourage you to find someone who both knows the best physical health practices and how to do inner work that will help you maintain your healthy habits.

Spirituality

When I refer to spirituality, I personally appreciate this definition:

> Your spirituality is the aspect of you that is tuned into the idea of there being something beyond you. In particular, being spiritual is about recognizing that our human senses don't tell the whole story about the universe. That there is more to us than our bodies and brains. Spirituality might involve endorsing a higher form of life or attributing some kind of conscious awareness to the universe.[1]

Spirituality does not require religious affiliation but can include it.

Research consistently shows that those who connect to spiritual practices report better well-being overall. One resource describes how more than 3,000 articles in scientific journals have been published on this topic and:

---

1 https://thelawofattraction.com/what-is-spirituality/. Accessed March 10, 2023.

> The available evidence underscores a generally positive effect between religion/spirituality (especially religious participation) and health variables, such as: minor depression, faster recovery from depressive episodes, lower rates of suicide, less use, abuse, and substance dependence, lower rate of coronary heart disease or hypertension, better functioning of the immune system, better functioning of the endocrine system, lower rates of cancer, better prognosis in cases of cancer, longevity, greater well-being and self-reported happiness (meaning of life, hope, optimism, forgiveness).[2]

Many people turn away from spirituality after experiencing hardships or injury from religious teachings and practices. If this has happened to you, I encourage you to seek resources that can help you navigate these spiritual wounds.

If you have turned away from spirituality or religion because you struggle to reconcile how tragic things can happen, I also encourage you to explore your spirituality. Trust me, I get how hard it is to believe in a greater "entity" that allows such pain and tragedy to exist in our world today. I, too, have had to navigate this road. What I found helpful is to find safe and trustworthy people, including spiritual leaders, who will support you in:

1. Voicing your pain associated with spirituality or religion.
2. Asking hard questions.
3. Learning how they navigated their own skepticism (or even rejection) of spirituality or religion.

Professional Resources

Your healing and growth journey can truly be optimized when you use professional resources. I advocate using a professional because the person

2 https://www.omicsonline.org/open-access/role-of-religion-and-spirituality-on-mental-health-and-resilience-there-is-enough-evidence-1522-4821-1000273.php?aid=61354. Accessed March 10, 2023.

commits to meeting you where you are and providing you the caring space to be fully vulnerable with the good, bad, and the messy in your life. They intentionally dedicate their time and energy to learning effective tools to help you move forward. Understanding and modifying human behavior is their specialty.

Psychotherapy with a Trained Clinician

Psychotherapy, most often referred to as therapy or counseling, is the process of participating in dialogue with a trained mental health professional to resolve mental health and interpersonal challenges. Psychotherapists obtain either a master's or doctoral degree, participate in several years of supervised clinical experience, and then obtain a license by meeting requirements set forth by state regulations. The most common psychotherapy licensures include:

- Licensed psychologist (PhD)
- Licensed marriage and family therapist
- Licensed clinical social worker
- Licensed professional counselor
- Licensed mental health counselor

These licensure tracks include training in many of the same areas, such as theories of human change and human development. However, they differ slightly in focus. For example, marriage and family therapists (such as myself) emphasize relationships and how to provide therapy concerning relationships. Psychologists often focus more on the individual psyche and conducting research on human behavior.

Licensed clinicians are trained to diagnosis mental health conditions (also referred to as mental illness, but I do not prefer this phrase) such as PTSD or major depressive disorder. This can be beneficial because with elevated symptoms meeting the criteria for a designated diagnosis, the therapist is trained in specific interventions to help improve the symptoms. They can also identify when medical intervention by a doctor might be beneficial.

If you decide to find a psychotherapist, the most important factors to consider are how well you connect with them and their choice of treatment modalities (described later in this chapter). Personality wise, you may resonate better with someone who is super-direct and doesn't sugarcoat things. Or you may feel more comfortable with someone who is gentler and provides a lot of praise. You may respond well to therapy with someone who assigns in-between session homework. Or you might prefer group therapy where you are with others who are working toward a similar goal or focusing on a similar problem. There are many options to explore.

If you have never been to therapy, it may take a little time to discover your preferences. Start with a phone consultation to ask how the therapy is structured and which treatment modalities are used. Get a feel for the therapist's personality to see if they might be someone you would want to work with. Attend a couple of sessions to see if you like the person and how they conduct the therapeutic process. Above all, no matter the therapist's style or techniques, your felt experience is most important. If you do not feel comfortable with them or feel they are not meeting your needs, speak up and request an adjustment or find someone new altogether.

Treatment Modalities to Consider

In the psychotherapy world, clinicians get trained in many treatment different modalities, each based on a theory of why people act the way they do, and the techniques to facilitate change. If you go to therapy, you don't necessarily need to know the exact models a therapist might use. At the same time, I want to suggest a few that could be beneficial for you to continue building on the tools in this book:

- Internal Family Systems Model (IFS): This model was developed by Richard Schwartz, PhD. IFS is based on a theoretical framework that we all have subpersonalities within our one person. The subpersonalities, otherwise known as "parts," function to ensure our safety and well-being.[3] You can deepen your understanding of your survival strategies by learning from and practicing the tools outlined by this model.

- Cognitive Behavior Therapy (CBT): This is the model described in Chapter 3 of this book that focuses on learning to modify your thoughts and subsequent behaviors. I suggest finding a therapist who integrates CBT throughout therapy alongside other models. There is a CBT model that specifically aims to heal trauma and is aptly called Trauma-Focused CBT. You can look for someone who has been specifically trained in this model.

- Eye Movement Desensitization and Reprocessing (EMDR): EMDR is a model that uses eye movement to process adverse experiences. It was created by Dr. Francine Shapiro. This treatment model shows some of the highest rates of efficacy in treating trauma and mental health symptoms.

  Twenty-four randomized, controlled trials support the positive effects of EMDR therapy in the treatment of emotional trauma and other adverse life experiences relevant to clinical practice. Seven of ten studies reported EMDR therapy to be more rapid and/or more effective than trauma-focused cognitive behavioral therapy. Twelve randomized studies of the eye movement component noted rapid decreases in negative emotions and/or vividness of disturbing images, with an additional eight reporting a variety of other memory effects. Numerous other evaluations document that EMDR therapy provides relief from a variety of somatic complaints.[4]

  For a clinician to provide EMDR treatment, they must go through a minimum of forty additional hours of specific training on top of

3 https://ifs-institute.com/. Accessed March 10, 2023.

4 https://www.ncbi.nlm.nih.gov/pmc/articles/PMC3951033/. Accessed March 10, 2023.

licensure. To learn more about EMDR, you can visit the EMDR International Association at emdria.org.

- Somatic Therapy: Somatic Therapy focuses on incorporating the body into your therapy. The therapist uses mind-body exercises to help the body release trauma and emotional charge.

  Rather than just talk about them, somatic therapists guide patients to focus on their underlying physical sensations. From there, the mind-body exercises may include breath work, meditation, visualization, massage, grounding, dance, and/or sensation awareness work.[5]

  Somatic Experiencing International has trademarked Somatic Experiencing™ based on Dr. Peter Levine's work. Many types of professionals, not just therapists, can get trained in this model. To become a certified practitioner, the professional must complete a three-year program. To learn more about the model or to find a certified somatic experiencing professional, go to:

  * https://traumahealing.org/
  * https://www.somaticexperiencing.com/somatic-experiencing

Coaching

Another professional support option is to hire a life coach. A life coach is someone who supports people in working toward specific goals. Generally, the goals focus on life enhancement such as elevating your career or improving personal health habits. Life coaches support you in aligning your everyday actions with your intended goals. You can hire a general life coach, or you can look for a coach whose niche fits your desired goals, such as a health coach or a business coach.

---

5 https://www.verywellmind.com/what-is-somatic-therapy-5190064. Accessed March 10, 2023.

Life coaching differs from psychotherapy in a few key areas. The first is that therapists are required to complete graduate school and complete the regimented state licensing processes. Life coaches can obtain specialty training to become a coach, but they are not required to. Life coaches are generally more focused on today's performance and goals for future performance. They do not delve into your past, while therapists often help you address your past to help make present-day changes. And last, coaches cannot treat mental health conditions.

I want to clarify that anyone can call themselves a life coach without any training. In addition, there is no regulatory oversight of coaching professionals like licensed professionals have. An organization called the International Coaching Federation exists to provide ethical guidelines for the coaching industry. However, no one is required to be involved with ICF. Phenomenal life coaches who have spent much time training to practice their craft and who practice ethically and with integrity are out there. At the same time, without regulation, the coaching industry can include coaches who can cause damage because they are not trained to help or because they don't follow ethical guidelines. Knowing this, if you feel that coaching could be a good fit for your growth journey, I recommend considering the following when hiring a coach:

1. What training do they have? Have they participated in any recognized programs to develop their craft as a coach? Is this training recognized by the International Coaching Federation?
2. How much experience do they have and what kind of experience?
3. What is their method of supporting clients?
4. Do they know and respect the boundaries of their coaching profession compared to a therapist?
5. What do they do to maintain their professional expertise?

A coach with integrity in providing services will eagerly answer these questions and will most often have the information readily available. I am personally trained through the Institute for Coaching Mastery, under the phenomenal coaching of Alyssa Nobriga. Her certification program is accredited through the International Coaching Federation.

It is common and acceptable to use both therapists and coaches, depending on the need and desired outcome. Sometimes you will have a future-focused goal in which a coach may provide more accountability and structure that could benefit you. Other times, you might engage in therapy to address the deeper-rooted issues that still need more extensive nurturing and exploration. If you want to use the support of both at the same time, just make sure each person knows about the other, and you are all clear about each professional's purpose.

Psychiatry/Medical Physician

Psychiatry is the medical branch that treats mental health conditions. A psychiatrist or psychiatric nurse practitioner assesses, diagnoses, and treats a patient with mental illness through medical intervention. More often than not, the medical intervention uses medications to alleviate symptoms. Primary care physicians or general practitioners are also trained to treat symptoms through medication, but psychiatrists specialize in diseases of the brain.

If you experience symptoms that meet the criteria for a mental health condition, medication is worth considering. I am not one to immediately suggest anyone see a psychiatrist. However, if symptoms are disrupting your daily functioning, I think it is better to include a medical professional to assess the symptoms and determine if medication or some other recommended form of treatment could be good for you.

Holistic Medicine

Holistic medicine is treatment that "considers the whole person—body, mind, spirit, and emotions—in the quest for optimal health and wellness. According to the holistic medicine philosophy, one can achieve optimal health—the primary goal of holistic medicine practice—by gaining proper balance in life."[6] Many holistic remedies originated in the east hemisphere of the globe and have been around for hundreds of years. Holistic treatment options include (but are not limited to):

- Acupuncture is the use of thin needles placed at strategic points of your body to treat pain, reduce stress, and promote overall wellness. It is often used to treat diseases and painful conditions such as fibromyalgia or headaches. You will want to ensure practitioners are credentialed to perform this treatment.[7]

- Meditation is the practice of calming down the mind. Many people hear "meditation" and think it means to sit silently for an hour and think of and do nothing. That is one way to meditate, but really meditation is any form of taking time to try to quiet the mind. It is more difficult at first when your mind is used to chattering all the time. However, the more you practice and find environmental ways to calm the mind, the easier it gets. I personally love doing guided meditations where someone is talking in a soothing voice, guiding me to notice my breath or use my imagination to relax my body. A resource I highly recommend is the app Insight Timer, which has thousands of meditations to choose from.

- Yoga is the practice of unifying the mind, body, and spirit. There are many different forms and practices of yoga such as movement through poses, breathing techniques, and meditation. Multiple studies suggest that yoga aids in the reduction of stress, improvement of health conditions, and awareness of mind-body connection.

- Reiki is an energy healing technique that aims to ease tension and stress in the body. It is done through the movement of the hands and gentle touch of the reiki practitioner. The purpose of a reiki

---

6 https://www.webmd.com/balance/guide/what-is-holistic-medicine. Accessed March 10, 2023.

7 https://www.mayoclinic.org/tests-procedures/acupuncture/about/pac-20392763. Accessed March 10, 2023.

session is to move energy fields within the body to promote the optimal flow of energy and remove blocks that can lead to illness or emotional distress. Research is limited on its effectiveness, but there are many reports of positive response.[8]

Be in Community

You are genetically a social creature. You are designed to thrive by connecting with others. Even if you have been hurt by others, I urge you to seek community in some form. Don't go at life, healing, and growth alone. One of the most astounding truths I have discovered for myself and witnessed in other people's lives is that healing and growth happen more fully and deeply when we join with others and allow others to support us. Independence can serve a purpose, but relationships have the power to heal the soul. Here are some ideas for finding community:

- Common interest groups such as a hiking or book club. Meetup.com has thousands of interest activity groups.
- Group therapy.
- Group coaching programs.
- Spiritual communities such as churches or meditation centers.
- Groups on social media with people who have common interests or values.

Growth Activity

Now that you have finished this book, I invite you to write a love letter to yourself. Celebrate yourself for doing the work to embody your worth. Declare your commitment to loving yourself and continue on your healing journey.

8 https://iarp.org/what-is-reiki/, https://www.reiki.org/faqs/what-reiki

A FINAL NOTE
I Hope You Dance

"Life's not about waiting for the storm to pass.
It's about learning to dance in the rain."
— Vivian Greene

When Ashton went straight to the NICU after birth, the nurses and doctors taught us an extremely important concept: "This is a marathon, not a sprint." They declared it imperative we take optimal care of ourselves so we could support Ashton long-term because they knew he would be sick for a while. They urged us to get proper sleep, take breaks, and eat meals regularly so we would not burn out and, consequently, not be able to show up at all for Ashton.

This analogy applies to your life as well. You are here for the marathon of life. During this marathon, you are going to encounter countless storms. Some will be small and pass by quickly. Others may be life-altering.

The loss of Ashton was not my first life-altering storm to conquer. Thank God I learned how to dance in the rain before he arrived. The most important dance I learned was the dance of being in love with myself, realizing how beautiful and worthy I am. This dance lesson gave me the trust that I would be okay no matter what the storm sent my way. To this day, I still know I will be okay.

Embrace your beauty. Gift yourself patience and compassion. Own your worth. Believe in your divine purpose. Pursue your dreams. Do all this so you can dance in the rain as it comes.

I wish you love and peace as you continue forward. *You* are *beyond worthy.*

References

Books

Burns, David. *The Feeling Good Handbook.* New, York, NY: Plume, 1990.

Cloud, Henry and John Townsend. *Boundaries: When to Say Yes, How to Say No to Take Control of Your Life*. Grand Rapids, MI: Zondervan, 1992.

Corey, Gerald. *Theories and Techniques of Counseling.* Belmont, CA: Brooks/Cole, 2005.

Haselton, M. G. et al. "The Evolution of Cognitive Bias." In *The Handbook of Evolutionary Psychology*. Ed. D. M. Buss. Hoboken, NJ: John Wiley & Sons, 2005.

Levine, Peter A. *Healing Trauma.* Boulder, CO: Sounds True, 2008.

Van der Kolk, Bessel. *The Body Keeps the Score*. New York, NY: Penguin, 2014.

Websites

"Brain meta-state transitions demarcate thoughts across task contexts exposing the mental noise of trait neuroticism." Nature.com.

"Discovery of 'thought worms' opens window to the mind." Medicalxpress.com.

https://drsuejohnson.com.

https://iarp.org/what-is-reiki/.

https://www.mayoclinic.org/tests-procedures/acupuncture/about/pac-20392763.

https://www.mirecc.va.gov/cih-visn2/Documents/Patient_Education_Handouts/Stress_Response_and_How_It_Can_Affect_You_Version_3.pdf.

https://www.ncbi.nlm.nih.gov/pmc/articles/PMC3621648/.

https://www.ncbi.nlm.nih.gov/pmc/articles/PMC3951033/.

https://www.nytimes.com/2017/06/08/smarter-living/benefits-of-talking-to-yourself-self-talk.html.

https://www.omicsonline.org/open-access/role-of-religion-and-spirituality-on-mental-health-and-resilience-there-is-enough-evidence-1522-4821-1000273.php?aid=61354.

https://www.psychologytoday.com/us/blog/anxiety-zen/201603/why-do-we-repeat-the-past-in-our-relationships.

https://www.reiki.org/faqs/what-reiki.

https://www.samhsa.gov/trauma-violence#.

https://www.verywellmind.com/what-is-somatic-therapy-5190064.

https://www.webmd.com/balance/guide/what-is-holistic-medicine.

https://www.webmd.com/mental-health/what-is-hypervigilance.

About the Author

Amanda Wallingsford is a licensed marriage and family therapist, board-approved supervisor, and life transformation coach. She completed her undergraduate education at Vanderbilt University, earning a Bachelor of Science with a major in Human and Organizational Development and a minor in Child Development. She earned her Master of Science in Counseling from San Diego State University.

Amanda has spent her entire career providing direct service to people struggling with mental health, adversity, or trauma. She has also held numerous positions of leadership to ensure program delivery meets best practice recommendations. She is equally passionate about working one-on-one with clients as she is contributing to the individual and organizational development of professionals in the helping fields.

Amanda is proud to be a wife, the mother of an angel, a stepmother to two amazing individuals, and a grandparent. She remains committed to being the best version of herself so she can positively impact her family, friends, clients, communities, and future generations.

Book Amanda Wallingsford to Speak or Lead at Your Next Event

When it comes to choosing a professional speaker or workshop leader for your next event, you absolutely want to book Amanda Wallingsford. She is sure to captivate and inspire your attendees.

Whether your audience is 10 or 10,000, in North America or abroad, Amanda Wallingsford can deliver a customized message of inspiration for your meeting or conference. Amanda understands your group does not want to be lectured to, but is rather interested in hearing stories of inspiration and learning tools that lead to true transformation.

Hire Amanda today for any of the following keynote speech or workshop topics:

- Claim Your Worth, Step into Your Power
- Turn Your Dreams into Reality
- Change Your Thoughts, Change Your Life
- Boundaries Set You Free
- Maximizing Your Communication
- Surviving Loss
- Beating Imposter Syndrome
- Recharge from Burnout
- Topic on demand (tailored to your community)

Amanda Wallingsford's speaking and leading philosophy is to speak from the heart, connect with the audience members through authenticity and vulnerability, and invite them to take their next most intelligent steps. If you are looking for a memorable speaker or workshop leader who will leave your community wanting more, book Amanda Wallingsford today!

To book Amanda for your event, email her at either address below to schedule a complimentary pre-event phone consultation:

Amanda@AlignAndEmbody.com

Align and Embody Coaching

Are you ready to *fully* embody your worth and create the life of your dreams? Are you ready to put these tools into action while receiving direct support from Amanda Wallingsford?

Amanda Wallingsford passionately offers various life transformation coaching packages to invite you into the best version of yourself. You have the option to choose between individual coaching that is tailored to your unique needs or join her signature group coaching program. The Embody Your Worth Group is a live, interactive coaching experience built as a hands-on extension of this book.

Based on her decades-long career supporting more than 1,500 individuals, Amanda uses her best coaching tools to help people align with their truth and embody their magnificence. Whether you are looking for guidance to tap into the vision of your dream life, expand your goals, execute your purpose-driven plan, or figure out how to get out of your own way, Amanda can support you. She works from the inside-out (inner experience to outer goal) because she knows the real power starts from within to create lasting change and transformation.

If you are interested in receiving coaching from Amanda, visit her website directly to schedule your clarity call or apply for the group program.

www.AlignAndEmbody.com

Amanda@AlignAndEmbody.com

Made in the USA
Middletown, DE
21 March 2024

51312285R00119